Precious Bible Promises

Also, known as Clarke's Scripture Promises

Compiled by Samuel Clarke, D.D. (1675-1729).

Reformatted by Tom Stewart

with

An Historical Perspective of *Precious Bible Promises*

by Tom Stewart

and

Notice by Dr. Isaac Watts (1674-1748)

Edited By Gregory A, White, 2011

Disclaimer and Terms of Use: The Author and Publisher has strived to be as accurate and complete as possible in the creation of this book, notwithstanding the fact that he does not warrant or represent at any time that the contents within are accurate due to the rapidly changing nature of the Internet. While all attempts have been made to verify information provided in this publication, the Author and Publisher assumes no responsibility for errors, omissions, or contrary interpretation of the subject matter herein. Any perceived slights of specific persons, peoples, or organizations are unintentional. In practical advice books, like anything else in life, there are no guarantees of income made. Readers are cautioned to reply on their own judgment about their individual circumstances to act accordingly. This book is not intended for use as a source of legal, business, accounting or financial advice. All readers are advised to seek services of competent professionals in legal, business, accounting, and finance field.

Table of Contents

An Historical Perspective of *Precious Bible Promises*

Samuel Clarke (1675-1729) was the compiler of this eminent book of *Precious Bible Promises* (1750). "Whereby are given unto us Exceeding Great and Precious Promises: that by these ye might be partakers of the Divine Nature" (2Peter 1:4). As an English academic, theologian, and preacher, Clarke would be found mastering Isaac Newton's new system of the Universal Laws of Motion and translating an invaluable textbook to introduce and promote Newton's position (1697), defending the Christian religion in *A Discourse concerning the Being and Attributes of God, the Obligations of Natural Religion, and the Truth and Certainly of the Christian Revelation* (1705), serving as a chaplain to Protestant Queen Anne of England (1705), translating Isaac Newton's *Optics* (1706), expounding upon the Tri-Unity of God in his celebrated treatise *The Scripture Doctrine of the Trinity* (1712), refusing the secular post of Master of the Mint (1727) upon the death of Sir Isaac Newton (whom he would have replaced), and accumulating ten volumes of his own sermons (published posthumously); but, best remembered by many Christians is his compilation of *Precious Bible Promises*, which shows us that Dr. Samuel Clarke had not only a keen intellect, but a true understanding of the evangelical "faith which worketh by love" (Galatians 5:6) and its attendant Promises. "Let him that glorieth glory in this, that he understandeth and knoweth Me, that I am the LORD which exercise lovingkindness, judgment, and righteousness, in the Earth: for in these things I delight, saith the LORD" (Jeremiah

9:24).

This book of *Precious Bible Promises* was once known by its 19th century readers as *Clarke's Scripture Promises*. Twenty-one years after the decease of Samuel Clarke, Isaac Watts, the Father of English Hymnology (1674-1748), penned the introduction to *Clarke's Scripture Promises*. In a time that already had seen the Authorized Version of the Scriptures from the Church of England-- the King James Version of 1611-- and had produced *The Pilgrim's Progress* (1675) from the Church of England's famous dissenter, John Bunyan (1628-1688)-- who was acquainted for twelve years with the hospitality of Bedford jail for preaching without a license-- a book of *Precious Bible Promises* was (and, still is needed) to encourage every True Believer in their pursuit of holy living. "Having therefore these Promises, dearly beloved, let us cleanse ourselves from all filthiness of the flesh and spirit, perfecting holiness in the fear of God" (2Corinthians 7:1). The "Notice by Dr. Watts" affixed to the front of the *Precious Bible Promises*, identifies Samuel Clarke as the "worthy author of this collection, which I ["I. Watts"] have known with esteem and honor." "I am a companion of all them that fear thee, and of them that keep thy precepts" (Psalm 119:63). Of interest, Isaac Watts, the author of over 600 hymns, was himself the son of another dissenter from the Church of England. You will probably notice that a good number of Clarke's compiled Promises were gleaned from the Book of Psalms of the Old Testament, and Watts could especially identify with their Promises, since he had himself published the *Psalms of David* (1719) in which are found poetic paraphrases of Psalm 90 ("O

God, Our Help in Ages Past") and Psalm 98 ("Joy to the World"). "10 The days of our years are threescore years and ten; and if by reason of strength they be fourscore years, yet is their strength labour and sorrow; for it is soon cut off, and we fly away. 17 And let the beauty of the LORD our God be upon us: and establish Thou the work of our hands upon us; yea, the work of our hands establish Thou it" (90:10, 17).

A notable 19th century advocate of *Clarke's Scripture Promises* was found in the person of the enigmatic, English General Charles G. Gordon (1833-1885)-- "Chinese Gordon," the "Hero of Khartoum," "Gordon Pasha." In January 1884, he had advised Lord Wolseley to distribute a copy of *Clarke's Scripture Promises* to every member of the Cabinet of Prime Minister William Gladstone upon Gordon's departure to handle the volatile situation of the revolting Mahdi in the Sudan. "Who through faith subdued kingdoms, wrought righteousness, obtained Promises, stopped the mouths of lions" (Hebrews 11:33). Charles Gordon had early made his peace with Jesus Christ as a young officer in the Royal Engineers at Pembroke (U.K.) after being pursued for Christ by his sister Augusta and by a "very religious captain of the name of Drew." "I will be merciful to their unrighteousness, and their sins and their iniquities will I remember no more" (8:12). Gordon had distinguished himself with conspicuous gallantry during the Crimean War (1853-1856), had successfully quelled the Taiping Rebellion in China (1863-1864), and had been instrumental in the suppression of the slave trade (1877-1880) in the Sudan (south of Egypt), during which he had been a solitary man of One Book-- his pocket Bible.

"Godliness is profitable unto all things, having Promise of the life that now is, and of that which is to come" (1Timothy 4:8). Though the career of General Gordon was peppered with the intensity of great overcoming in times of conflict, he knew times of obscurity and grievous backsliding; but, as he once wrote to his sister Augusta, "I am glad to say that this disease [a smallpox experienced in China] has brought me back to my Saviour, and I trust in future to be a better Christian than I have been hitherto." "Whom the LORD loveth He chasteneth, and scourgeth every son whom He receiveth" (Hebrews 12:6). In the timing of God's Providence, Gordon Pasha met his end on the morning of January 26th 1885, two days before the British relief column reached the newly subjugated city of Khartoum, where the unbowing Gordon had held out to the end. "Ye shall be hated of all men for My Name's sake: but he that endureth to the end shall be saved" (Matthew 10:22).

Rosalind Goforth, a Canadian Christian missionary, was another who lived in 19th century China that gave a glowing recommendation of the value of *Clarke's Scripture Promises.* She wrote of the faithfulness of God in her testimonial book, *How I Know God Answers Prayer.* "They shall abundantly utter the memory of Thy great goodness" (Psalm 145:7). As she, her husband Jonathan, and her four children faced the bloody onslaught of the anti-foreigner, anti-Christian Boxer Revolt of the secret society "Harmonious Fists" of China (1900), they were advised by the American Consul in Chefoo to flee from the city of Changte in North Honan to the coastal seaport of Shanghai. "No weapon that is formed against thee shall prosper" (Isaiah 54:17). On the morning of July 8th 1900, their small party of missionaries was resting at an inn in the small town of Hsintien, while a boisterous mob awaited them outside casting stones and demanding their money. Rosalind wrote,

> "Hints had been given us of coming danger, but that was all; none spoke of what all felt -- that we were probably going to our death. Suddenly, without the slightest warning, I was seized with an overwhelming fear of what might be awaiting us. It was not the fear of *after* death, but of probable torture, that took such awful hold of me. I thought, 'Can this be the Christian courage I have looked for?' I went by myself and prayed for victory, but no help came. Just then someone called us to a room for prayer before getting into our carts. Scarcely able to walk for trembling, and utterly ashamed that others should see my state of panic -- for such it undoubtedly was -- I managed to reach a bench beside which my husband stood. He drew from his pocket a little book, *Clarke's Scripture Promises*, and read the verses his eyes first fell upon. They were the following:
>
> The eternal God is thy refuge, and underneath are the everlasting arms: and he shall thrust out the enemy from before thee; and shall say, Destroy them.
> The God of Jacob is our refuge.

Thou art my help and my deliverer; make no tarrying, O my God.
I will strengthen thee; yea, I will help thee; yea, I will uphold thee with the right hand of my righteousness... The Lord thy God will hold thy right hand, saying unto thee, Fear not; I will help thee.
If God be for us, who can be against us?
We may boldly say, The Lord is my helper, and I will not fear what man shall do unto me.

The effect of these words at such a time was remarkable. All realized that God was speaking to us. Never was there a message more directly given to mortal man from his God than that message to us. From almost the first verse my whole soul seemed flooded with a great peace; all trace of panic vanished; and I felt God's presence was with us. Indeed, His presence was so real it could scarcely have been more so had we seen a visible form."

Needless to say, they all escaped with their lives with each able to give amazing stories of physical deliverance from innumerable attempts to kill, injure, or maim them. "Who delivered us from so great a death, and doth deliver: in Whom we trust that He will yet deliver us" (2Corinthians 1:10).

The testimony from the past serves to remind us that the same

God Who Promised Abraham that He would make him a father of a great multitude-- which He did-- has Promised us, "Call unto Me, and I will answer thee, and shew thee great and mighty things, which thou knowest not" (Jeremiah 33:3). May we be like Abraham in rising to the challenge. "20 He staggered not at the Promise of God through unbelief; but was strong in Faith, giving Glory to God; 21 And being fully persuaded that, what He had Promised, He was able also to perform" (Romans 4:20-21).

May God bless you as you lay hold of His Promises!

Tom Stewart
"Thy Counsels of old are Faithfulness and Truth" (Isaiah 25:1).
November 15th 2003

Notice by Dr. Isaac Watts (1674-1748)

The Bible is a book of such transcendent worth, and so happily suited to all the parts and purposes of the Christian life, that it can never be too much recommended to the world; every thing that allures the world to peruse it, is a blessing to mankind. And though it is hard for our narrow capacities to grasp and take in its several distinguishing excellences at one view, yet, if we take a separate survey of the doctrines and duties, the promises and threatenings, the prophecies and histories, which are contained therein, each of them will afford us an awful or a delightful prospect, with lessons for special improvement.

The worthy author of this collection, which I have long known with esteem and honor, has chosen to reduce all the most useful and important promises of the Word of God into order, and here set them before us. These are the most powerful motives of duty; these are the constant food of a living Christian, as well as his highest cordials in a fainting hour. And in such a world as this, where duties perpetually demand our practice, and difficulties and trials are ever surrounding us, what can we do better than to treasure up the promises in our hearts, which are the most effectual persuasives to fulfil the one and sustain the other? Here are laid up the true riches of a Christian, and his highest hopes on this side of heaven.

The materials which are collected here are all divine, and the disposition of them is elegant and regular; so that it is an easy matter to find something suited to the frame of our souls, or our present wants on every occasion; and that soul who knows what a suitable promise is worth in an hour of darkness or temptation, will never think such a work as this, and such a various treasure, can have sufficient value set upon it.

Those who have little leisure for reading, may find their account in keeping this book always near them; and with the glance of an eye they may take in the riches of grace and glory, and derive many a sweet refreshment from hence, amidst their labors and travels through this wilderness. It is of excellent use to lie on the table in a chamber of sickness, and now and then to take a sip of the river of life, which runs through it in a thousand little rills of peace and joy.

May the Holy Spirit of God, who indited all these promises, and our blessed Mediator, who, by his ministry and by his blood, has sealed and confirmed them all, render them every day more and more powerful and prevalent to draw the hearts of men towards God, and to fit them for the enjoyment of these words of grace in their complete accomplishment in glory. Amen.

I. Watts
Newington, Jan. 19, 1750

"PRECIOUS BIBLE PROMISES"

PART ONE

BLESSINGS PROMISED TO BELIEVERS

Chapter 1

Promises Of Temporal Blessings

1. General Promises To Believers

"The LORD God is a sun and shield: the LORD will give grace and glory: no good thing will he withhold from them that walk uprightly" (Psalm 84:11).

"The lines are fallen unto me in pleasant places; yea, I have a goodly heritage" (Psalm 16:6).

"Surely I know that it shall be well with them that fear God, which fear before him" (Ecclesiastes 8:12).

"Say ye to the righteous, that it shall be well with him: for they shall eat the fruit of their doings" (Isaiah 3:10).

"Verily there is a reward for the righteous" (Psalm 58:11).

"Thou, LORD, wilt bless the righteous; with favour wilt thou compass him as with a shield" (Psalm 5:12).

"Salvation belongeth unto the LORD: thy blessing is upon thy people" (Psalm 3:8).

"He that followeth after righteousness and mercy findeth life, righteousness, and honour" (Proverbs 21:21).

"Blessings are upon the head of the just. The desire of the righteous shall be granted. The hope of the righteous shall be gladness" (Proverbs 10:6, 24, 28).

"To him that soweth righteousness shall be a sure reward. Righteousness tendeth to life. The righteous shall flourish as a branch. (Proverbs 11:18, 19, 28).

"His secret is with the righteous" (Proverbs 3:32).

"A good man obtaineth favour of the LORD" (Proverbs 12:2).

"The light of the righteous rejoiceth. To the righteous good shall be repayed" (Proverbs 13:9, 21).

"Surely goodness and mercy shall follow me all the days of my life: and I will dwell in the house of the LORD for ever" (Psalm 23:6).

"He that spared not his own Son, but delivered him up for us all, how shall he not with him also freely give us all things?" (Romans 8:32).

"All things are yours; whether Paul, or Apollos, or Cephas, or the world, or life, or death, or things present, or things to come; all are yours" (1Corinthians 3:21, 22).

"Godliness is profitable unto all things, having promise of the life that now is, and of that which is to come" (1Timothy 4:8).

2. Temporal Blessings In General

"The LORD is my shepherd; I shall not want. Thou preparest a table before me in the presence of mine enemies: thou anointest my head with oil; my cup runneth over" (Psalm 23:1, 5).

"There is no want to them that fear him. They that seek the LORD shall not want any good thing" (Psalms 34:9, 10).

"Seek ye first the kingdom of God, and his righteousness; and all these things shall be added unto you" (Matthew 6:33).

"My God shall supply all your need according to his riches in glory by Christ Jesus" (Philippians 4:19).

"Godliness with contentment is great gain. Who giveth us richly all things to enjoy" (1Timothy 6:6, 17).

3. Food And Raiment

Food

"Trust in the LORD, and do good; so shalt thou dwell in the land, and verily thou shalt be fed" (Psalm 37:3).

"He hath given meat unto them that fear him: he will ever be mindful of his covenant" (Psalm 111:5).

"I will abundantly bless her provision: I will satisfy her poor with bread" (Psalm 132:15).

"He filleth thee with the finest of the wheat" (Psalm 147:14).

"The righteous eateth to the satisfying of his soul" (Proverbs 13:25).

"26 Behold the fowls of the air: for they sow not, neither do they reap, nor gather into barns; yet your heavenly Father feedeth them. Are ye not much better than they?" (Matthew 6:26).

"And ye shall eat in plenty, and be satisfied" (Joel 2:26).

"Behold, my servants shall eat, but ye shall be hungry: behold, my servants shall drink, but ye shall be thirsty" (Isaiah 65:13).

Raiment

"I say unto you, Take no thought for your life, what ye shall eat, or what ye shall drink; nor yet for your body, what ye shall put on. Is not the life more than meat, and the body than raiment? Wherefore, if God so clothe the grass of the field, which to day is, and to morrow is cast into the oven, shall he not much more clothe you, O ye of little faith? Therefore take no thought, saying, What shall we eat? or, What shall we drink? or, Wherewithal shall we be clothed? For your heavenly Father knoweth that ye have need of all these things" (Matthew 6:25, 30, 31, 32).

4. Long Life And Health

Long Life

"Ye shall walk in all the ways which the LORD your God hath commanded you, that ye may live, and that it may be well with you, and that ye may prolong your days in the land which ye shall possess" (Deuteronomy 5:33).

"That thou mightest fear the LORD thy God, to keep all his statutes and his commandments, which I command thee, thou, and thy son, and thy son's son, all the days of thy life; and that thy days may be prolonged" (Deuteronomy 6:2).

"Thou shalt come to thy grave in a full age, like as a shock of corn cometh in his season" (Job 5:26).

"What man is he that desireth life, and loveth many days, that he may see good? Keep thy tongue from evil, and thy lips from speaking guile. Depart from evil, and do good; seek peace, and pursue it" (Psalm 34:12-14).

"With long life will I satisfy him, and shew him my salvation" (Psalm 91:16).

"Length of days, and long life, and peace, shall they add to thee. Length of days is in her [Wisdom's] right hand" (Proverbs 3:2, 16).

"By me thy days shall be multiplied, and the years of thy life shall be increased" (Proverbs 9:11).

Health

"Who forgiveth all thine iniquities; who healeth all thy diseases; Who redeemeth thy life from destruction; who crowneth thee with lovingkindness and tender mercies; Who satisfieth thy mouth with good things; so that thy youth is renewed like the eagle's" (Psalm 103:3-5).

"Be not wise in thine own eyes: fear the LORD, and depart from evil. It shall be health to thy navel, and marrow to thy bones" (Proverbs 3:7, 8).

"They are life unto those that find them, and health to all their flesh" (Proverbs 4:22).

5. Safety Under The Divine Protection

"The beloved of the LORD shall dwell in safety by him; and the LORD shall cover him all the day long" (Deuteronomy 33:12).

"The name of the LORD is a strong tower: the righteous runneth into it, and is safe" (Proverbs 18:10).

"I have set the LORD always before me: because he is at my right hand, I shall not be moved" (Psalm 16:8).

"He shall not be afraid of evil tidings: his heart is fixed, trusting in the LORD" (Psalm 112:7).

"And who is he that will harm you, if ye be followers of that which is good?" (1Peter 3:13).

"Remember, I pray thee, who ever perished, being innocent? or where were the righteous cut off?" (Job 4:7).

"Thou shalt be secure, because there is hope" (Job 11:18).

"Thou shalt be in league with the stones of the field: and the beasts of the field shall be at peace with thee" (Job 5:23).

"And in that day will I make a covenant for them with the beasts of the field, and with the fowls of heaven, and with the creeping things of the ground: and I will break the bow and the sword and the battle out of the earth, and will make them to lie down safely" (Hosea 2:18).

"I will make with them a covenant of peace, and will cause the evil beasts to cease out of the land: and they shall dwell safely in the wilderness, and sleep in the woods. And they shall no more be a prey to the heathen, neither shall the beast of the land devour them; but they shall dwell safely, and none shall make them afraid" (Ezekiel 34:25, 28).

"And the fear of you and the dread of you shall be upon every beast of the earth, and upon every fowl of the air, upon all that moveth upon the earth, and upon all the fishes of the sea; into your hand are they delivered" (Genesis 9:2).

"Thou shalt dig about thee, and thou shalt take thy rest in safety. Also thou shalt lie down, and none shall make thee afraid" (Job 11:18, 19).

"I will both lay me down in peace, and sleep: for thou, LORD, only makest me dwell in safety" (Psalm 4:8).

"He giveth his beloved sleep" (Psalm 127:2).

"When thou liest down, thou shalt not be afraid: yea, thou shalt lie down, and thy sleep shall be sweet" (Proverbs 3:24).

"He will keep the feet of his saints, and the wicked shall be silent in darkness; for by strength shall no man prevail" (1Samuel 2:9).

"The LORD is my light and my salvation; whom shall I fear? the LORD is the strength of my life; of whom shall I be afraid?" (Psalm 27:1).

"He keepeth all his bones: not one of them is broken" (Psalm 34:20).

"He that dwelleth in the secret place of the most High shall abide under the shadow of the Almighty. I will say of the LORD, He is my refuge and my fortress: my God; in him will I trust. He shall cover thee with his feathers, and under his wings shalt thou trust: his truth shall be thy shield and buckler. There shall no evil befall thee, neither shall any plague come nigh thy dwelling" (Psalm 91:1, 2, 4, 10).

"I will lift up mine eyes unto the hills, from whence cometh my help. My help cometh from the LORD, which made heaven and earth. He will not suffer thy foot to be moved: he that keepeth thee will not slumber. Behold, he that keepeth Israel shall neither slumber nor sleep. The LORD is thy keeper: the LORD is thy shade upon thy right hand. The sun shall not smite thee by day, nor the moon by night. The LORD shall preserve thee from all evil: he shall preserve thy soul. The LORD shall preserve thy going out and thy coming in from this time forth, and even for evermore" (Psalm 121:1-8).

"Our help is in the name of the LORD, who made heaven and earth" (Psalm 124:8).

"As the mountains are round about Jerusalem, so the LORD is round about his people from henceforth even for ever" (Psalm 125:2).

"Then shalt thou walk in thy way safely, and thy foot shall not stumble" (Proverbs 3:23).

"But whoso hearkeneth unto me shall dwell safely, and shall be quiet from fear of evil" (Proverbs 1:33).

"And the LORD will create upon every dwelling place of mount Zion, and upon her assemblies, a cloud and smoke by day, and the shining of a flaming fire by night: for upon all the glory shall be a defence. And there shall be a tabernacle for a shadow in the daytime from the heat, and for a place of refuge, and for a covert from storm and from rain" (Isaiah 4:5, 6).

"He shall dwell on high: his place of defence shall be the munitions of rocks" (Isaiah 33:16).

"When thou passest through the waters, I will be with thee; and through the rivers, they shall not overflow thee: when thou walkest through the fire, thou shalt not be burned; neither shall the flame kindle upon thee. For I am the LORD thy God, the Holy One of Israel, thy Saviour" (Isaiah 43:2, 3).

"I the LORD do keep it; I will water it every moment: lest any hurt it, I will keep it night and day" (Isaiah 27:3).

"For I, saith the LORD, will be unto her a wall of fire round about, and will be the glory in the midst of her" (Zechariah 2:5).

6. Promises Of Peace

"And I will give peace in the land, and ye shall lie down, and none shall make you afraid: and I will rid evil beasts out of the land, neither shall the sword go through your land" (Leviticus 26:6).

"The LORD will give strength unto his people; the LORD will bless his people with peace" (Psalm 29:11).

"Peace shall be upon Israel" (Psalm 125:5).

"Great peace have they which love thy law: and nothing shall offend them" (Psalm 119:165).

"He maketh peace in thy borders" (Psalm 147:14).

"LORD, thou wilt ordain peace for us: for thou also hast wrought all our works in us" (Isaiah 26:12).

"My people shall dwell in a peaceable habitation, and in sure dwellings, and in quiet resting places" (Isaiah 32:18).

7. Direction

"The steps of a good man are ordered by the LORD: and he delighteth in his way" (Psalm 37:23).

"He will be our guide even unto death" (Psalm 48:14).

"Thou shalt guide me with thy counsel, and afterward receive me to glory" (Psalm 73:24).

"In all thy ways acknowledge him, and he shall direct thy paths" (Proverbs 3:6).

"The righteousness of the perfect shall direct his way" (Proverbs 11:5).

"A man's heart deviseth his way: but the LORD directeth his steps" (Proverbs 16:9).

"His God doth instruct him to discretion, and doth teach him" (Isaiah 28:26).

"And I will bring the blind by a way that they knew not; I will lead them in paths that they have not known: I will make darkness light before them, and crooked things straight. These things will I do unto them, and not forsake them" (Isaiah 42:16).

8. Honor

"And the LORD shall make thee the head, and not the tail; and thou shalt be above only, and thou shalt not be beneath; if that thou hearken unto the commandments of the LORD thy God, which I command thee this day, to observe and to do them" (Deuteronomy 28:13).

"Surely he shall not be moved for ever: the righteous shall be in everlasting remembrance. his horn shall be exalted with honour" (Psalm 112:6, 9).

"For them that honour me I will honour" (1Samuel 2:30).

"By humility and the fear of the LORD are riches, and honour, and life" (Proverbs 22:4).

"In her left hand riches and honour" (Proverbs 3:16).

"Exalt her, and she shall promote thee: she shall bring thee to honour, when thou dost embrace her" (Proverbs 4:8).

"The memory of the just is blessed" (Proverbs 10:7).

"Because he hath set his love upon me, therefore will I deliver him: I will set him on high, because he hath known my name. He shall call upon me, and I will answer him: I will be with him in trouble; I will deliver him, and honour him" (Psalm 91:14, 15).

"If any man serve me, let him follow me; and where I am, there shall also my servant be: if any man serve me, him will my Father honour" (John 12:26).

"Behold, I will make them of the synagogue of Satan, which say they are Jews, and are not, but do lie; behold, I will make them to come and worship before thy feet, and to know that I have loved thee" (Revelation 3:9).

9. Success And Prosperity

"He shall be like a tree planted by the rivers of water, that bringeth forth his fruit in his season; his leaf also shall not wither; and whatsoever he doeth shall prosper" (Psalm 1:3).

"Commit thy way unto the LORD; trust also in him; and he shall bring it to pass" (Psalm 37:5).

"Thou shalt eat the labour of thine hands: happy shalt thou be, and it shall be well with thee" (Psalm 128:2).

"I will cry unto God most high; unto God that performeth all things for me" (Psalm 57:2).

"And they shall build houses, and inhabit them; and they shall plant vineyards, and eat the fruit of them. They shall not build, and another inhabit; they shall not plant, and another eat: for as the days of a tree are the days of my people, and mine elect shall long enjoy the work of their hands. They shall not labour in vain, nor bring forth for trouble; for they are the seed of the blessed of the LORD, and their offspring with them" (Isaiah 65:21-23).

"Thou shalt be stedfast, and shalt not fear: 16 Because thou shalt forget thy misery, and remember it as waters that pass away: And thine age shall be clearer than the noonday; thou shalt shine forth, thou shalt be as the morning" (Job 11:15, 17).

"Thou shalt also decree a thing, and it shall be established unto thee: and the light shall shine upon thy ways" (Job 22:28).

10. Plenty And Riches

"I will give you the rain of your land in his due season, the first rain and the latter rain, that thou mayest gather in thy corn, and thy wine, and thine oil. And I will send grass in thy fields for thy cattle, that thou mayest eat and be full" (Deuteronomy 11:14, 15).

"The LORD shall open unto thee his good treasure, the heaven to give the rain unto thy land in his season, and to bless all the work of thine hand: and thou shalt lend unto many nations, and thou shalt not borrow" (Deuteronomy 28:12).

"And the LORD thy God will make thee plenteous in every work of thine hand, in the fruit of thy body, and in the fruit of thy cattle, and in the fruit of thy land, for good: for the LORD will again rejoice over thee for good, as he rejoiced over thy fathers. And the LORD shall make thee plenteous in goods, in the fruit of thy body, and in the fruit of thy cattle, and in the fruit of thy ground, in the land which the LORD sware unto thy fathers to give thee" (Deuteronomy 30:9; 28:11).

"Then shalt thou lay up gold as dust, and the gold of Ophir as the stones of the brooks. Yea, the Almighty shall be thy defence, and thou shalt have plenty of silver" (Job 22:24, 25).

"He blesseth them also, so that they are multiplied greatly; and suffereth not their cattle to decrease" (Psalm 107:38).

"Wealth and riches shall be in his house: and his righteousness endureth for ever" (Psalm 112:3).

"In her [Wisdom's] left hand riches and honour" (Proverbs

3:16).

"Riches and honour are with me; yea, durable riches and righteousness. My fruit is better than gold, yea, than fine gold; and my revenue than choice silver" (Proverbs 8:18, 19).

"In the house of the righteous is much treasure" (Proverbs 15:6).

"Then shall he give the rain of thy seed, that thou shalt sow the ground withal; and bread of the increase of the earth, and it shall be fat and plenteous: in that day shall thy cattle feed in large pastures" (Isaiah 30:23).

11. Of Children

"He will love thee, and bless thee, and multiply thee: he will also bless the fruit of thy womb" (Deuteronomy 7:13).

"And the LORD thy God will make thee plenteous in every work of thine hand, in the fruit of thy body" (Deuteronomy 30:9).

"Thou shalt know also that thy seed shall be great, and thine offspring as the grass of the earth" (Job 5:25).

"Lo, children are an heritage of the LORD: and the fruit of the womb is his reward. As arrows are in the hand of a mighty man; so are children of the youth. Happy is the man that hath his quiver full of them: they shall not be ashamed, but they shall speak with the enemies in the gate" (Psalm 127:3-5).

"The LORD shall increase you more and more, you and your

children" (Psalm 115:14).

12. A Blessing Upon All The Believer Has

"And ye shall serve the LORD your God, and he shall bless thy bread, and thy water" (Exodus 23:25).

"And thou shalt rejoice in every good thing which the LORD thy God hath given unto thee, and unto thine house" (Deuteronomy 26:11).

"Blessed shalt thou be in the city, and blessed shalt thou be in the field. Blessed shall be the fruit of thy body, and the fruit of thy ground, and the fruit of thy cattle, the increase of thy kine, and the flocks of thy sheep. Blessed shall be thy basket and thy store. Blessed shalt thou be when thou comest in, and blessed shalt thou be when thou goest out. The LORD shall command the blessing upon thee in thy storehouses, and in all that thou settest thine hand unto; and he shall bless thee in the land which the LORD thy God giveth thee" (Deuteronomy 28:3-6, 8).

"A little that a righteous man hath is better than the riches of many wicked" (Psalm 37:16).

"The blessing of the LORD, it maketh rich, and he addeth no sorrow with it" (Proverbs 10:22).

"Better is little with the fear of the LORD than great treasure and trouble therewith" (Proverbs 15:16).

"For God giveth to a man that is good in his sight wisdom, and knowledge, and joy: but to the sinner he giveth travail, to gather and to heap up, that he may give to him that is good before God" (Ecclesiastes 2:26).

"Every man should eat and drink, and enjoy the good of all his labour, it is the gift of God" (Ecclesiastes 3:13).

"Every man also to whom God hath given riches and wealth, and hath given him power to eat thereof, and to take his portion, and to rejoice in his labour; this is the gift of God. For he shall not much remember the days of his life; because God answereth him in the joy of his heart" (Ecclesiastes 5:19, 20).

13. A Blessing Upon The Children Of Believers

"Thou shalt keep therefore his statutes, and his commandments, which I command thee this day, that it may go well with thee, and with thy children after thee, and that thou mayest prolong thy days upon the earth, which the LORD thy God giveth thee, for ever. O that there were such an heart in them, that they would fear me, and keep all my commandments always, that it might be well with them, and with their children for ever!" (Deuteronomy 4:40; 5:29).

"A good man leaveth an inheritance to his children's children: and the wealth of the sinner is laid up for the just" (Proverbs 13:22).

"In the fear of the LORD is strong confidence: and his children shall have a place of refuge" (Proverbs 14:26).

"The seed of the righteous shall be delivered" (Proverbs 11:21).

"The just man walketh in his integrity: his children are blessed after him" (Proverbs 20:7).

"The children of thy servants shall continue, and their seed shall be established before thee." (Psalm 102:28).

"His seed shall be mighty upon earth: the generation of the upright shall be blessed" (Psalm 112:2).

"His seed shall inherit the earth" (Psalm 25:13).

"I have been young, and now am old; yet have I not seen the righteous forsaken, nor his seed begging bread. He is ever merciful, and lendeth; and his seed is blessed" (Psalm 37:25, 26).

"He hath blessed thy children within thee" (Psalm 147:13).

"I will give them one heart, and one way, that they may fear me for ever, for the good of them, and of their children after them" (Jeremiah 32:39).

14. A Blessing Upon The Families Of The Good

"Thou shalt know that thy tabernacle shall be in peace; and thou shalt visit thy habitation, and shalt not sin" (Job 5:24).

"If thou wert pure and upright; surely now he would awake for thee, and make the habitation of thy righteousness prosperous. Though thy beginning was small, yet thy latter end should greatly increase" (Job 8:6, 7).

"Thy wife shall be as a fruitful vine by the sides of thine house:

thy children like olive plants round about thy table. Behold, that thus shall the man be blessed that feareth the LORD. The LORD shall bless thee out of Zion: and thou shalt see the good of Jerusalem all the days of thy life. Yea, thou shalt see thy children's children, and peace upon Israel" (Psalm 128:3-6).

"He blesseth the habitation of the just" (Proverbs 3:33).

"The house of the righteous shall stand" (Proverbs 12:7).

"The tabernacle of the upright shall flourish" (Proverbs 14:11).

Chapter 2
Promises Relating To The Troubles Of Life

1. In General

Preservation From Trouble

"For this shall every one that is godly pray unto thee in a time when thou mayest be found: surely in the floods of great waters they shall not come nigh unto him. Thou art my hiding place; thou shalt preserve me from trouble; thou shalt compass me about with songs of deliverance" (Psalm 32:6, 7).

"He shall deliver thee in six troubles: yea, in seven there shall no evil touch thee" (Job 5:19).

"The LORD preserveth the faithful" (Psalm 31:23).

"There shall no evil befall thee, neither shall any plague come nigh thy dwelling" (Psalm 91:10).

"There shall no evil happen to the just" (Proverbs 12:21).

"The way of the slothful man is as an hedge of thorns: but the way of the righteous is made plain" (Proverbs 15:19).

Deliverance From Trouble

"Behold, God will not cast away a perfect man, neither will he help the evil doers: Till he fill thy mouth with laughing, and thy lips with rejoicing. (Job 8:20, 21).

"Thou shalt forget thy misery, and remember it as waters that pass away" (Job 11:16).

"Even so would he have removed thee out of the strait into a broad place, where there is no straitness; and that which should be set on thy table should be full of fatness" (Job 36:16).

"For his anger endureth but a moment; in his favour is life: weeping may endure for a night, but joy cometh in the morning" (Psalm 30:5).

"Many are the afflictions of the righteous: but the LORD delivereth him out of them all" (Psalm 34:19).

"Why art thou cast down, O my soul? and why art thou disquieted within me? hope thou in God: for I shall yet praise him, who is the health of my countenance, and my God" (Psalm 42:11).

"Though ye have lien among the pots, yet shall ye be as the wings of a dove covered with silver, and her feathers with yellow gold" (Psalm 68:13).

"Thou, which hast shewed me great and sore troubles, shalt quicken me again, and shalt bring me up again from the depths of the earth" (Psalm 71:20).

"For thou wilt save the afflicted people; but wilt bring down high looks. For thou wilt light my candle: the LORD my God will enlighten my darkness" (Psalm 18:27, 28).

"The LORD openeth the eyes of the blind: the LORD raiseth them that are bowed down" (Psalm 146:8).

"They cry unto the LORD in their trouble, and he saveth them out of their distresses" (Psalm 107:19).

"They that sow in tears shall reap in joy. He that goeth forth and weepeth, bearing precious seed, shall doubtless come again with rejoicing, bringing his sheaves with him" (Psalm 126:5, 6).

"The righteous is delivered out of trouble, and the wicked cometh in his stead" (Proverbs 11:8).

"The wicked is snared by the transgression of his lips: but the just shall come out of trouble" (Proverbs 12:13).

"For a just man falleth seven times, and riseth up again" (Proverbs 24:16).

"I know the thoughts that I think toward you, saith the LORD, thoughts of peace, and not of evil, to give you an expected end" (Jeremiah 29:11).

"Their soul shall be as a watered garden; and they shall not sorrow any more at all. I will turn their mourning into joy, and will comfort them, and make them rejoice from their sorrow" (Jeremiah 31:12, 13).

"Come, and let us return unto the LORD: for he hath torn, and he will heal us; he hath smitten, and he will bind us up" (Hosea 6:1).

Support In Trouble

"The LORD also will be a refuge for the oppressed, a refuge in times of trouble" (Psalm 9:9).

"He hath not despised nor abhorred the affliction of the afflicted; neither hath he hid his face from him; but when he cried unto him, he heard" (Psalm 22:24).

"When my father and my mother forsake me, then the LORD will take me up. Wait on the LORD: be of good courage, and he shall strengthen thine heart: wait, I say, on the LORD" (Psalm 27:10, 14).

"Though he fall, he shall not be utterly cast down: for the LORD upholdeth him with his hand. The salvation of the righteous is of the LORD: he is their strength in the time of trouble" (Psalm 37:24, 39).

"The LORD is my rock, and my fortress, and my deliverer; my God, my strength, in whom I will trust; my buckler, and the horn of my salvation, and my high tower" (Psalm 18:2).

"God is our refuge and strength, a very present help in trouble. 2 Therefore will not we fear, though the earth be removed, and though the mountains be carried into the midst of the sea; though the waters thereof roar and be troubled, though the mountains shake with the swelling thereof. Selah" (Psalm 46:1-3).

"Cast thy burden upon the LORD, and he shall sustain thee: he shall never suffer the righteous to be moved" (Psalm 55:22).

"I will be glad and rejoice in thy mercy: for thou hast considered my trouble; thou hast known my soul in adversities" (Psalm 31:7).

"I have surely seen the affliction of my people which are in Egypt, and have heard their cry by reason of their taskmasters; for I know their sorrows" (Exodus 3:7).

"Blessed is he that considereth the poor: the LORD will deliver him in time of trouble" (Psalm 41:1).

"Thou hast given commandment to save me; for thou art my rock and my fortress" (Psalm 71:3).

"Unto the upright there ariseth light in the darkness" (Psalm 112:4).

"Who remembered us in our low estate: for his mercy endureth for ever" (Psalm 136:23).

"Though I walk in the midst of trouble, thou wilt revive me: thou shalt stretch forth thine hand against the wrath of mine enemies, and thy right hand shall save me" (Psalm 138:7).

"My flesh and my heart faileth: but God is the strength of my heart" (Psalm 73:26).

"The LORD upholdeth all that fall, and raiseth up all those that be bowed down" (Psalm 145:14).

"Thou hast been a strength to the poor, a strength to the needy in his distress, a refuge from the storm, a shadow from the heat, when the blast of the terrible ones is as a storm against the wall" (Isaiah 25:4).

"In measure, when it shooteth forth, thou wilt debate with it: he stayeth his rough wind in the day of the east wind" (Isaiah 27:8).

"He will not lay upon man more than right; that he should enter into judgment with God" (Job 34:23).

"Who is among you that feareth the LORD, that obeyeth the voice of his servant, that walketh in darkness, and hath no light? let him trust in the name of the LORD, and stay upon his God" (Isaiah 50:10).

"For the Lord will not cast off for ever: But though he cause grief, yet will he have compassion according to the multitude of his mercies. For he doth not afflict willingly nor grieve the children of men" (Lamentations 3:31-33).

"O LORD, my strength, and my fortress, and my refuge in the day of affliction" (Jeremiah 16:19).

"I am with thee, saith the LORD, to save thee: though I make a full end of all nations whither I have scattered thee, yet will I not make a full end of thee: but I will correct thee in measure, and will not leave thee altogether unpunished" (Jeremiah 30:11).

"Rejoice not against me, O mine enemy: when I fall, I shall arise; when I sit in darkness, the LORD shall be a light unto me. I will bear the indignation of the LORD, because I have sinned against him, until he plead my cause, and execute judgment for me: he will bring me forth to the light, and I shall behold his righteousness" (Micah 7:8, 9).

"The LORD is good, a strong hold in the day of trouble; and he knoweth them that trust in him" (Nahum 1:7).

"Come unto me, all ye that labour and are heavy laden, and I will give you rest" (Matthew 11:28).

"These things I have spoken unto you, that in me ye might have peace. In the world ye shall have tribulation: but be of good cheer; I have overcome the world" (John 16:33).

"For as the sufferings of Christ abound in us, so our consolation also aboundeth by Christ" (2Corinthians 1:5).

"We are troubled on every side, yet not distressed; we are perplexed, but not in despair; Persecuted, but not forsaken; cast down, but not destroyed" (2Corinthians 4:8, 9).

2. Promises Relating To Sickness, Old Age, Etc.

Deliverance From Sickness

"Ye shall serve the LORD your God, and he shall bless thy bread, and thy water; and I will take sickness away from the midst of thee" (Exodus 23:25).

"If thou wilt diligently hearken to the voice of the LORD thy God, and wilt do that which is right in his sight, and wilt give ear to his commandments, and keep all his statutes, I will put none of these diseases upon thee, which I have brought upon the Egyptians: for I am the LORD that healeth thee" (Exodus

15:26).

"He is gracious unto him, and saith, Deliver him from going down to the pit: I have found a ransom. His flesh shall be fresher than a child's: he shall return to the days of his youth: He shall pray unto God, and he will be favourable unto him: and he shall see his face with joy: for he will render unto man his righteousness. He will deliver his soul from going into the pit, and his life shall see the light" (Job 33:24-26, 28).

"Surely he shall deliver thee from the snare of the fowler, and from the noisome pestilence. Thou shalt not be afraid for the terror by night; nor for the arrow that flieth by day; Nor for the pestilence that walketh in darkness; nor for the destruction that wasteth at noonday" (Psalm 91:3, 5, 6).

"Who forgiveth all thine iniquities; who healeth all thy diseases" (Psalm 103:3).

"The LORD will take away from thee all sickness, and will put none of the evil diseases of Egypt, which thou knowest, upon thee" (Deuteronomy 7:15).

"Behold, I will bring it health and cure, and I will cure them, and will reveal unto them the abundance of peace and truth" (Jeremiah 33:6).

Support In Sickness

"The LORD will strengthen him upon the bed of languishing: thou wilt make all his bed in his sickness" (Psalm 41:3).

"The LORD preserveth the simple: I was brought low, and he helped me" (Psalm 116:6).

"Notwithstanding she shall be saved in childbearing, if they continue in faith and charity and holiness with sobriety" (1Timothy 2:15).

"He will also bless the fruit of thy womb" (Deuteronomy 7:13).

"Even by the God of thy father, who shall help thee; and by the Almighty, who shall bless thee with blessings of heaven above, blessings of the deep that lieth under, blessings of the breasts, and of the womb" (Genesis 49:25).

In Old Age

"Cast me not off in the time of old age; forsake me not when my strength faileth" (Psalm 71:9).

"And even to your old age I am he; and even to hoar hairs will I carry you: I have made, and I will bear; even I will carry, and will deliver you" (Isaiah 46:4).

"The hoary head is a crown of glory, if it be found in the way of righteousness" (Proverbs 16:31).

3. Deliverance From Famine And Want

"In famine he shall redeem thee from death. At destruction and famine thou shalt laugh" (Job 5:20, 22).

"Behold, the eye of the LORD is upon them that fear him, upon them that hope in his mercy; to deliver their soul from death, and to keep them alive in famine" (Psalm 33:18, 19).

"They shall not be ashamed in the evil time: and in the days of famine they shall be satisfied" (Psalm 37:19).

"Which giveth food to the hungry" (Psalm 146:7).

"When the poor and needy seek water, and there is none, and their tongue faileth for thirst, I the LORD will hear them, I the God of Israel will not forsake them" (Isaiah 41:17).

"I will call for the corn, and will increase it, and lay no famine upon you. And I will multiply the fruit of the tree, and the increase of the field, that ye shall receive no more reproach of famine among the heathen" (Ezekiel 36:29, 30).

"Ask ye of the LORD rain in the time of the latter rain; so the LORD shall make bright clouds, and give them showers of rain, to every one grass in the field" (Zechariah 10:1).

"He satisfieth the longing soul, and filleth the hungry soul with goodness" (Psalm 107:9).

"Although the fig tree shall not blossom, neither shall fruit be in the vines; the labour of the olive shall fail, and the fields shall yield no meat; the flock shall be cut off from the fold, and there shall be no herd in the stalls: Yet I will rejoice in the LORD, I will joy in the God of my salvation" (Habakkuk 3:17, 18).

"Man shall not live by bread alone, but by every word that proceedeth out of the mouth of God" (Matthew 4:4).

4. Deliverance from war and enemies

From War

"The LORD your God is he that goeth with you, to fight for you against your enemies, to save you. For the LORD thy God walketh in the midst of thy camp, to deliver thee, and to give up thine enemies before thee; therefore shall thy camp be holy: that he see no unclean thing in thee, and turn away from thee" (Deuteronomy 20:4; 23:14).

"In war from the power of the sword" (Job 5:20).

"Through God we shall do valiantly: for he it is that shall tread down our enemies" (Psalm 60:12).

"Behold, God himself is with us for our captain" (2Chronicles 13:12).

"Be not afraid of sudden fear, neither of the desolation of the wicked, when it cometh. For the LORD shall be thy confidence, and shall keep thy foot from being taken" (Proverbs 3:25, 26).

"Behold, all they that were incensed against thee shall be ashamed and confounded: they shall be as nothing; and they that strive with thee shall perish. Thou shalt seek them, and shalt not find them, even them that contended with thee: they that war against thee shall be as nothing, and as a thing of nought" (Isaiah 41:11, 12).

"I will deliver thee in that day, saith the LORD: and thou shalt not be given into the hand of the men of whom thou art afraid. For I will surely deliver thee, and thou shalt not fall by the sword, but thy life shall be for a prey unto thee: because thou hast put thy trust in me, saith the LORD" (Jeremiah 39:17, 18).

From Enemies

"Fear not: for they that be with us are more than they that be with them" (2Kings 6:16).

"LORD, it is nothing with thee to help, whether with many, or with them that have no power" (2Chronicles 14:11).

"The LORD your God ye shall fear; and he shall deliver you out of the hand of all your enemies" (2Kings 17:39).

"Shew thy marvellous lovingkindness, O thou that savest by thy right hand them which put their trust in thee from those that rise up against them" (Psalm 17:7).

"In the time of trouble he shall hide me in his pavilion: in the secret of his tabernacle shall he hide me; he shall set me up upon a rock. And now shall mine head be lifted up above mine enemies round about me: therefore will I offer in his tabernacle sacrifices of joy; I will sing, yea, I will sing praises unto the LORD" (Psalm 27:5, 6).

"The wicked watcheth the righteous, and seeketh to slay him. The LORD will not leave him in his hand, nor condemn him when he is judged. And the LORD shall help them, and deliver them: he shall deliver them from the wicked, and save them, because they trust in him" (Psalm 37:32, 33, 40).

"He preserveth the souls of his saints; he delivereth them out of the hand of the wicked" (Psalm 97:10).

"His heart is established, he shall not be afraid, until he see his desire upon his enemies" (Psalm 112:8).

"The LORD taketh my part with them that help me: therefore shall I see my desire upon them that hate me" (Psalm 118:7).

"The rod of the wicked shall not rest upon the lot of the righteous; lest the righteous put forth their hands unto iniquity" (Psalm 125:3).

"They that hate thee shall be clothed with shame; and the dwelling place of the wicked shall come to nought" (Job 8:22).

"When a man's ways please the LORD, he maketh even his enemies to be at peace with him" (Proverbs 16:7).

"Thou shalt bring down the noise of strangers, as the heat in a dry place; even the heat with the shadow of a cloud: the branch of the terrible ones shall be brought low" (Isaiah 25:5).

"Whosoever shall gather together against thee shall fall for thy sake. No weapon that is formed against thee shall prosper; and every tongue that shall rise against thee in judgment thou shalt condemn. This is the heritage of the servants of the LORD, and their righteousness is of me, saith the LORD" (Isaiah 54:15, 17).

"The LORD shall cause thine enemies that rise up against thee to be smitten before thy face: they shall come out against thee one way, and flee before thee seven ways" (Deuteronomy 28:7).

"Shall not God avenge his own elect, which cry day and night unto him, though he bear long with them? I tell you that he will avenge them speedily" (Luke 18:7, 8).

"I am with thee, and no man shall set on thee to hurt thee" (Acts 18:10).

"So that we may boldly say, The Lord is my helper, and I will not fear what man shall do unto me. The LORD is on my side; I will not fear: what can man do unto me?" (Hebrews 13:6; Psalm 118:6).

"That we should be saved from our enemies, and from the hand of all that hate us; That he would grant unto us, that we being delivered out of the hand of our enemies might serve him without fear, in holiness and righteousness before him, all the days of our life" (Luke 1:71, 74, 75).

5. From Oppression And Injustice

"If thou at all take thy neighbour's raiment to pledge, thou shalt deliver it unto him by that the sun goeth down: For that is his covering only, it is his raiment for his skin: wherein shall he sleep? and it shall come to pass, when he crieth unto me, that I will hear; for I am gracious" (Exodus 22:26, 27).

"For the oppression of the poor, for the sighing of the needy, now will I arise, saith the LORD; I will set him in safety from him that puffeth at him" (Psalm 12:5).

"All my bones shall say, LORD, who is like unto thee, which deliverest the poor from him that is too strong for him, yea, the poor and the needy from him that spoileth him?" (Psalm 35:10).

"He shall judge the poor of the people, he shall save the children of the needy, and shall break in pieces the oppressor. He shall redeem their soul from deceit and violence: and precious shall their blood be in his sight" (Psalm 72:4, 14).

"He shall stand at the right hand of the poor, to save him from those that condemn his soul" (Psalm 109:31).

"Which executeth judgment for the oppressed" (Psalm 146:7).

"If thou seest the oppression of the poor, and violent perverting of judgment and justice in a province, marvel not at the matter: for he that is higher than the highest regardeth; and there be higher than they" (Ecclesiastes 5:8).

"In righteousness shalt thou be established: thou shalt be far from oppression; for thou shalt not fear: and from terror; for it shall not come near thee" (Isaiah 54:14).

6. From Slander And Reproach

Slander

"Thou shalt be hid from the scourge of the tongue: neither shalt thou be afraid of destruction when it cometh" (Job 5:21).

"Thou lift up thy face without spot" (Job 11:15).

"He shall bring forth thy righteousness as the light, and thy judgment as the noonday" (Psalm 37:6).

"Thou shalt hide them in the secret of thy presence from the pride of man: thou shalt keep them secretly in a pavilion from the strife of tongues" (Psalm 31:20).

"He shall send from heaven, and save me from the reproach of him that would swallow me up. Selah. God shall send forth his mercy and his truth" (Psalm 57:3).

Reproach

"Hearken unto me, ye that know righteousness, the people in whose heart is my law; fear ye not the reproach of men, neither be ye afraid of their revilings. For the moth shall eat them up like a garment, and the worm shall eat them like wool: but my righteousness shall be for ever, and my salvation from generation to generation" (Isaiah 51:7, 8).

"Blessed are ye, when men shall revile you, and persecute you, and shall say all manner of evil against you falsely, for my sake. Rejoice, and be exceeding glad: for great is your reward in heaven" (Matthew 5:11, 12).

"Esteeming the reproach of Christ greater riches than the treasures in Egypt: for he had respect unto the recompence of the reward" (Hebrews 11:26).

"If ye be reproached for the name of Christ, happy are ye; for the spirit of glory and of God resteth upon you: on their part he is evil spoken of, but on your part he is glorified" (1Peter 4:14).

7. From Witchcraft

"Surely there is no enchantment against Jacob, neither is there any divination against Israel" (Numbers 23:23).

8. Promises To The Stranger And The Exile

"He loveth the stranger, in giving him food and raiment" (Deuteronomy 10:18).

"The LORD preserveth the strangers" (Psalm 146:9).

"Thus saith the Lord GOD; Although I have cast them far off among the heathen, and although I have scattered them among the countries, yet will I be to them as a little sanctuary in the countries where they shall come" (Ezekiel 11:16).

9. To The Poor And Helpless

"The needy shall not alway be forgotten: the expectation of the poor shall not perish for ever" (Psalm 9:18).

"Thou, O God, hast prepared of thy goodness for the poor" (Psalm 68:10).

"The LORD heareth the poor" (Psalm 69:33).

"I will satisfy her poor with bread" (Psalm 132:15).

"The firstborn of the poor shall feed, and the needy shall lie down in safety" (Isaiah 14:30).

"He shall judge thy people with righteousness, and thy poor with judgment. He shall deliver the needy when he crieth; the poor also, and him that hath no helper. He shall spare the poor and needy, and shall save the souls of the needy" (Psalm 72:2, 12, 13).

"He will regard the prayer of the destitute, and not despise their prayer" (Psalm 102:17).

"Yet setteth he the poor on high from affliction, and maketh him families like a flock" (Psalm 107:41).

"He raiseth up the poor out of the dust, and lifteth the needy out of the dunghill" (Psalm 113:7).

"Sing unto the LORD, praise ye the LORD: for he hath delivered the soul of the poor from the hand of evildoers" (Jeremiah 20:13).

"He saveth the poor from the sword, from their mouth, and from the hand of the mighty. So the poor hath hope, and iniquity stoppeth her mouth" (Job 5:15, 16).

"He delivereth the poor in his affliction, and openeth their ears in oppression" (Job 36:15).

"Let the brother of low degree rejoice in that he is exalted" (James 1:9).

"Hearken, my beloved brethren, Hath not God chosen the poor of this world rich in faith, and heirs of the kingdom which he hath promised to them that love him?" (James 2:5).

"Abraham said, Son, remember that thou in thy lifetime receivedst thy good things, and likewise Lazarus evil things: but now he is comforted, and thou art tormented" (Luke 16:25).

10. To The Fatherless And Widow

"Ye shall not afflict any widow, or fatherless child. If thou afflict them in any wise, and they cry at all unto me, I will surely hear their cry; and my wrath shall wax hot, and I will kill you with the sword; and your wives shall be widows, and your children fatherless" (Exodus 22:22-24).

"He doth execute the judgment of the fatherless and widow" (Deuteronomy 10:18).

"The poor committeth himself unto thee; thou art the helper of the fatherless. To judge the fatherless and the oppressed, that the man of the earth may no more oppress" (Psalm 10:14, 18).

"A father of the fatherless, and a judge of the widows, is God in his holy habitation" (Psalm 68:5).

"He relieveth the fatherless and widow" (Psalm 146:9).

"The LORD will destroy the house of the proud: but he will establish the border of the widow" (Proverbs 15:25).

"Remove not the old landmark; and enter not into the fields of the fatherless: 11 For their Redeemer is mighty; he shall plead their cause with thee" (Proverbs 23:10, 11).

"Leave thy fatherless children, I will preserve them alive; and let thy widows trust in me" (Jeremiah 49:11).

"In thee the fatherless findeth mercy" (Hosea 14:3).

11. To The Childless

"God setteth the solitary in families" (Psalm 68:6).

"He maketh the barren woman to keep house, and to be a joyful mother of children" (Psalm 113:9).

"Thus saith the LORD unto the eunuchs that keep my Sabbaths, and choose the things that please me, and take hold of my covenant; even unto them will I give in mine house and within my walls a place and a name better than of sons and of daughters: I will give them an everlasting name, that shall not be cut off" (Isaiah 56:4, 5).

12. To The Prisoner And Captive

"He bringeth out those which are bound with chains" (Psalm 68:6).

"The LORD looseth the prisoners" (Psalm 146:7).

"If any of thine be driven out unto the outmost parts of heaven, from thence will the LORD thy God gather thee, and from thence will he fetch thee" (Deuteronomy 30:4).

"He despiseth not his prisoners" (Psalm 69:33).

"[He] brought them out of darkness and the shadow of death, and brake their bands in sunder" (Psalm 107:14).

"The captive exile hasteneth that he may be loosed, and that he should not die in the pit, nor that his bread should fail" (Isaiah 51:14).

"Thus saith the LORD, Even the captives of the mighty shall be taken away, and the prey of the terrible shall be delivered: for I will contend with him that contendeth with thee, and I will save thy children" (Isaiah 49:25).

"Verily it shall be well with thy remnant; verily I will cause the enemy to entreat thee well in the time of evil and in the time of affliction" (Jeremiah 15:11).

13. Deliverance From Death

"He will deliver his soul from going into the pit, and his life shall see the light" (Job 33:28).

"He that is our God is the God of salvation; and unto GOD the Lord belong the issues from death" (Psalm 68:20).

"O bless our God, ye people, and make the voice of his praise to be heard: which holdeth our soul in life, and suffereth not our feet to be moved" (Psalms 66:8, 9).

"From heaven did the LORD behold the earth; to hear the groaning of the prisoner; to loose those that are appointed to death" (Psalm 102:19, 20).

"Their soul abhorreth all manner of meat; and they draw near unto the gates of death. Then they cry unto the LORD in their trouble, and he saveth them out of their distresses" (Psalm 107:18, 19).

"Precious in the sight of the LORD is the death of his saints" (Psalm 116:15).

"A thousand shall fall at thy side, and ten thousand at thy right hand; but it shall not come nigh thee" (Psalm 91:7).

"Thou that liftest me up from the gates of death" (Psalm 9:13).

"The LORD killeth, and maketh alive: he bringeth down to the grave, and bringeth up" (1Samuel 2:6).

"See now that I, even I, am he, and there is no god with me: I kill, and I make alive; I wound, and I heal: neither is there any that can deliver out of my hand" (Deuteronomy 32:39).

Chapter 3

Promises Of Spiritual Blessings In This Life

1. In General

"All the paths of the LORD are mercy and truth unto such as keep his covenant and his testimonies. The secret of the LORD is with them that fear him; and he will shew them his covenant" (Psalm 25:10, 14).

"Blessed be the God and Father of our Lord Jesus Christ, who hath blessed us with all spiritual blessings in heavenly places in Christ: according as he hath chosen us in him before the foundation of the world, that we should be holy and without blame before him in love: according to the riches of his grace; wherein he hath abounded toward us in all wisdom and prudence" (Ephesians 1:3, 4, 7, 8).

"According as his divine power hath given unto us all things that pertain unto life and godliness, through the knowledge of Him that hath called us to glory and virtue: whereby are given unto us exceeding great and precious promises" (2Peter 1:3, 4).

"As many as walk according to this rule, peace be on them, and mercy, and upon the Israel of God" (Galatians 6:16).

"Whom he did predestinate, them he also called: and whom he called, them he also justified: and whom he justified, them he also glorified" (Romans 8:30).

2. Of Justification, Pardon, And Reconciliation

Justification

"He hath not beheld iniquity in Jacob, neither hath he seen perverseness in Israel" (Numbers 23:21).

"In the LORD shall all the seed of Israel be justified, and shall glory" (Isaiah 45:25).

"By his knowledge shall my righteous servant justify many; for he shall bear their iniquities" (Isaiah 53:11).

"Then will I sprinkle clean water upon you, and ye shall be clean: from all your filthiness, and from all your idols, will I cleanse you" (Ezekiel 36:25).

"Being justified freely by his grace through the redemption that is in Christ Jesus" (Romans 3:24).

"There is therefore now no condemnation to them which are in Christ Jesus, who walk not after the flesh, but after the Spirit. Who shall lay any thing to the charge of God's elect? It is God that justifieth. Who is he that condemneth? It is Christ that died, yea rather, that is risen again, who is even at the right hand of God, who also maketh intercession for us" (Romans 8:1, 33, 34).

"That being justified by his grace, we should be made heirs according to the hope of eternal life" (Titus 3:7).

"He hath made him to be sin for us, who knew no sin; that we might be made the righteousness of God in him" (2Corinthians 5:21).

"By him all that believe are justified from all things, from which ye could not be justified by the law of Moses" (Acts 13:39).

"Being justified by faith, we have peace with God through our Lord Jesus Christ. Being now justified by his blood, we shall be saved from wrath through him. By the righteousness of one the free gift came upon all men unto justification of life. So by the obedience of one shall many be made righteous" (Romans 5:1, 9, 18, 19).

Pardon Of Sin

"Keeping mercy for thousands, forgiving iniquity and transgression and sin" (Exodus 34:7).

"As for our transgressions, thou shalt purge them away" (Psalm 65:3).

"I, even I, am he that blotteth out thy transgressions for mine own sake, and will not remember thy sins" (Isaiah 43:25).

"There is forgiveness with thee, that thou mayest be feared. He shall redeem Israel from all his iniquities" (Psalm 130:4, 8).

"The inhabitant shall not say, I am sick: the people that dwell therein shall be forgiven their iniquity" (Isaiah 33:24).

"I have blotted out, as a thick cloud, thy transgressions, and, as a cloud, thy sins: return unto me; for I have redeemed thee" (Isaiah

44:22).

"He will not always chide: neither will he keep his anger for ever. He hath not dealt with us after our sins; nor rewarded us according to our iniquities. For as the heaven is high above the earth, so great is his mercy toward them that fear him. As far as the east is from the west, so far hath he removed our transgressions from us" (Psalm 103:9-12).

"Mine heart is turned within me, my repentings are kindled together. I will not execute the fierceness of mine anger, I will not return to destroy Ephraim" (Hosea 11:8, 9).

"Who is a God like unto thee, that pardoneth iniquity, and passeth by the transgression of the remnant of his heritage? He retaineth not his anger for ever, because he delighteth in mercy. He will turn again, he will have compassion upon us; he will subdue our iniquities; and thou wilt cast all their sins into the depths of the sea" (Micah 7:18, 19).

"Their sins and iniquities will I remember no more" (Hebrews 10:17).

"I will forgive their iniquity, and I will remember their sin no more" (Jeremiah 31:34).

"I will be merciful to their unrighteousness, and their sins and their iniquities will I remember no more" (Hebrews 8:12).

"Her sins, which are many, are forgiven; for she loved much. And he said unto her, Thy sins are forgiven. Thy faith hath saved thee; go in peace" [See Repentance, part 2, chap. 1, sect. 2] (Luke 7:47, 48, 50).

"All manner of sin and blasphemy shall be forgiven unto men: but the blasphemy against the Holy Ghost shall not be forgiven unto men. And whosoever speaketh a word against the Son of man, it shall be forgiven him" (Matthew 12:31, 32).

"Blessed is he whose transgression is forgiven, whose sin is covered. Blessed is the man unto whom the LORD imputeth not iniquity, and in whose spirit there is no guile" (Psalm 32:1, 2).

Of The Most Heinous Sins

"Though your sins be as scarlet, they shall be as white as snow; though they be red like crimson, they shall be as wool" (Isaiah 1:18).

Of All Sins

"Who forgiveth all thine iniquities; who healeth all thy diseases" (Psalm 103:3).

"I will cleanse them from all their iniquity, whereby they have sinned against me; and I will pardon all their iniquities, whereby they have sinned, and whereby they have transgressed against me" (Jeremiah 33:8).

"None of his sins that he hath committed shall be mentioned unto him" (Ezekiel 33:16).

Of Backsliding

"Return, thou backsliding Israel, saith the LORD; and I will not cause mine anger to fall upon you. Return, ye backsliding children, and I will heal your backslidings" (Jeremiah 3:12, 22).

"I will heal their backsliding, I will love them freely" (Hosea 14:4).

Pardon Through Christ

"In that day there shall be a fountain opened to the house of David and to the inhabitants of Jerusalem for sin and for uncleanness" (Zechariah 13:1).

"He shall save his people from their sins" (Matthew 1:21).

"Through this man is preached unto you the forgiveness of sins" (Acts 13:38).

"In whom we have redemption through his blood, the forgiveness of sins, according to the riches of his grace" (Ephesians 1:7).

"Who gave himself for our sins" (Galatians 1:4).

"This is a faithful saying, and worthy of all acceptation, that Christ Jesus came into the world to save sinners" (1Timothy 1:15).

"Christ died for our sins according to the Scriptures" (1Corinthians 15:3).

"When he had by himself purged our sins" (Hebrews 1:3).

"He hath appeared to put away sin by the sacrifice of himself. Christ was once offered to bear the sins of many" (Hebrews 9:26, 28).

"By one offering he hath perfected for ever them that are sanctified" (Hebrews 10:14).

"The Lamb of God, which taketh away the sin of the world" (John 1:29).

"This is my blood of the new testament, which is shed for many for the remission of sins" (Matthew 26:28).

"He was wounded for our transgressions, he was bruised for our iniquities: the chastisement of our peace was upon him; and with his stripes we are healed. All we like sheep have gone astray; we have turned every one to his own way; and the LORD hath laid on him the iniquity of us all" (Isaiah 53:5, 6).

"If any man sin, we have an advocate with the Father, Jesus Christ the righteous: He is the propitiation for our sins: and not for ours only, but also for the sins of the whole world. I write unto you, little children, because your sins are forgiven you for his name's sake" (1John 2:1, 12).

"The blood of Jesus Christ his Son cleanseth us from all sin. If we confess our sins, he is faithful and just to forgive us our sins, and to cleanse us from all unrighteousness" (1John 1:7, 9).

"He was manifested to take away our sins" (1John 3:5).

"Who his own self bare our sins in his own body on the tree, that we, being dead to sins, should live unto righteousness: by whose stripes ye were healed" (1Peter 2:24).

"That loved us, and washed us from our sins in his own blood" (Revelation 1:5).

Reconciliation

"Let him take hold of my strength, that he may make peace with me; and he shall make peace with me" (Isaiah 27:5).

"Being now justified by his blood, we shall be saved from wrath through him. For if, when we were enemies, we were reconciled to God by the death of his Son, much more, being reconciled, we shall be saved by his life" (Romans 5:9, 10).

"All things are of God, who hath reconciled us to himself by Jesus Christ, and hath given to us the ministry of reconciliation; to wit, that God was in Christ, reconciling the world unto himself, not imputing their trespasses unto them" (2Corinthians 5:18, 19).

"Now in Christ Jesus ye who sometimes were far off are made nigh by the blood of Christ. For he is our peace, who hath made both one, and hath broken down the middle wall of partition between us; having abolished in his flesh the enmity, even the law of commandments contained in ordinances; for to make in himself of twain one new man, so making peace; and that he might reconcile both unto God in one body by the cross, having slain the enmity thereby: and came and preached peace to you which were afar off, and to them that were nigh" (Ephesians

2:13-17).

"You, that were sometime alienated and enemies in your mind by wicked works, yet now hath he reconciled in the body of his flesh through death, to present you holy and unblameable and unreproveable in his sight: if ye continue in the faith grounded and settled, and be not moved away from the hope of the gospel, which ye have heard, and which was preached to every creature which is under heaven" (Colossians 1:21-23).

"A merciful and faithful high priest in things pertaining to God, to make reconciliation for the sins of the people" (Hebrews 2:17).

3. Adoption

"I am a Father to Israel, and Ephraim is my firstborn" (Jeremiah 31:9).

"Doubtless thou art our father, though Abraham be ignorant of us, and Israel acknowledge us not: thou, O LORD, art our father, our redeemer; thy name is from everlasting" (Isaiah 63:16).

"But now, O LORD, thou art our father; we are the clay, and thou our potter; and we all are the work of thy hand" (Isaiah 64:8).

"As many as are led by the Spirit of God, they are the sons of God. For ye have not received the spirit of bondage again to fear; but ye have received the Spirit of adoption, whereby we cry, Abba, Father" (Romans 8:14, 15).

"And it shall come to pass, that in the place where it was said unto them, Ye are not my people; there shall they be called the children of the living God" (Romans 9:26).

"[I] will be a Father unto you, and ye shall be my sons and daughters, saith the Lord Almighty" (2Corinthians 6:18).

"Ye are all the children of God by faith in Christ Jesus" (Galatians 3:26).

"God sent forth his Son, to redeem them that were under the law, that we might receive the adoption of sons. Wherefore thou art no more a servant, but a son; and if a son, then an heir of God through Christ" (Galatians 4:4, 5, 7).

"Having predestinated us unto the adoption of children by Jesus Christ to himself, according to the good pleasure of his will, to the praise of the glory of his grace, wherein he hath made us accepted in the Beloved" (Ephesians 1:5, 6).

"As many as received him, to them gave he power to become the sons of God, even to them that believe on his name" (John 1:12).

"Behold, what manner of love the Father hath bestowed upon us, that we should be called the sons of God. Beloved, now are we the sons of God" (1John 3:1, 2).

4. Union And Communion With The Church

"Ye are come unto mount Sion, and unto the city of the living God, the heavenly Jerusalem, and to an innumerable company of angels, to the general assembly and church of the firstborn, which are written in heaven, and to God the Judge of all, and to the spirits of just men made perfect, and to Jesus the mediator of the new covenant, and to the blood of sprinkling, that speaketh better things than that of Abel" (Hebrews 12:22-24).

"For we are the circumcision, which worship God in the spirit, and rejoice in Christ Jesus" (Philippians 3:3).

"There is neither Jew nor Greek, there is neither bond nor free, there is neither male nor female: for ye are all one in Christ Jesus. And if ye be Christ's, then are ye Abraham's seed, and heirs according to the promise" (Galatians 3:28, 29).

"Jerusalem which is above is free, which is the mother of us all. Now we, brethren, as Isaac was, are the children of promise" (Galatians 4:26, 28).

"That which we have seen and heard declare we unto you, that ye also may have fellowship with us: and truly our fellowship is with the Father, and with his Son Jesus Christ" (1John 1:3).

"That at that time ye were without Christ, being aliens from the commonwealth of Israel, and strangers from the covenants of promise, having no hope, and without God in the world: but now in Christ Jesus ye who sometimes were far off are made nigh by the blood of Christ. Now therefore ye are no more strangers and foreigners, but fellowcitizens with the saints, and of the household of God; in whom [Christ] ye also are builded together for an habitation of God through the Spirit" (Ephesians 2:12, 13, 19, 22).

"Thou, being a wild olive tree, wert graffed in among them, and with them partakest of the root and fatness of the olive tree" (Romans 11:17).

5. Free Access To God, With Acceptance

"Through him we both have access by one Spirit unto the Father" (Ephesians 2:18).

"In mine holy mountain will I accept them, and there will I require your offerings. I will accept you with your sweet savour" (Ezekiel 20:40, 41).

"In whom we have boldness and access with confidence by the faith of him" (Ephesians 3:12).

"Having therefore, brethren, boldness to enter into the holiest by the blood of Jesus, by a new and living way, which he hath consecrated for us, through the veil, that is to say, his flesh" (Hebrews 10:19, 20).

"Wherein he hath made us accepted in the Beloved" (Ephesians 1:6).

"To whom coming, as unto a living stone, disallowed indeed of men, but chosen of God, and precious, ye also, as lively stones, are built up a spiritual house, an holy priesthood, to offer up spiritual sacrifices, acceptable to God by Jesus Christ" (1Peter 2:4, 5).

6. Of Hearing Prayer

"Thou shalt make thy prayer unto him, and he shall hear thee" (Job 22:27).

"But know that the LORD hath set apart him that is godly for himself: the LORD will hear when I call unto him" (Psalm 4:3).

"This poor man cried, and the LORD heard him, and saved him out of all his troubles. The eyes of the LORD are upon the righteous, and his ears are open unto their cry. The righteous cry, and the LORD heareth, and delivereth them out of all their troubles" (Psalm 34:6, 15, 17).

"Call upon me in the day of trouble: I will deliver thee, and thou shalt glorify me" (Psalm 50:15).

"O thou that hearest prayer, unto thee shall all flesh come" (Psalm 65:2).

"He shall call upon me, and I will answer him" (Psalm 91:15).

"He will fulfil the desire of them that fear him: he also will hear their cry, and will save them" (Psalm 145:19).

"The LORD is far from the wicked: but he heareth the prayer of the righteous" (Proverbs 15:29).

"He will be very gracious unto thee at the voice of thy cry; when he shall hear it, he will answer thee" (Isaiah 30:19).

"Then shalt thou call, and the LORD shall answer; thou shalt cry, and he shall say, Here I am" (Isaiah 58:9).

"And it shall come to pass, that before they call, I will answer; and while they are yet speaking, I will hear" (Isaiah 65:24).

"Then shall ye call upon me, and ye shall go and pray unto me, and I will hearken unto you" (Jeremiah 29:12).

"They shall call on my name, and I will hear them: I will say, It is my people: and they shall say, The LORD is my God" (Zechariah 13:9).

"Ask, and it shall be given you; seek, and ye shall find; knock, and it shall be opened unto you: for every one that asketh receiveth; and he that seeketh findeth; and to him that knocketh it shall be opened. If ye then, being evil, know how to give good gifts unto your children, how much more shall your Father which is in heaven give good things to them that ask him?" (Matthew 7:7, 8, 11).

"And all things, whatsoever ye shall ask in prayer, believing, ye shall receive" (Matthew 21:22).

"If ye abide in me, and my words abide in you, ye shall ask what ye will, and it shall be done unto you" (John 15:7).

"And in that day ye shall ask me nothing. Verily, verily, I say unto you, Whatsoever ye shall ask the Father in my name, he will give it you. Hitherto have ye asked nothing in my name: ask, and ye shall receive, that your joy may be full" (John 16:23, 24).

"And whatsoever ye shall ask in my name, that will I do, that the Father may be glorified in the Son. If ye shall ask any thing in my name, I will do it" (John 14:13, 14).

"And the prayer of faith shall save the sick, and the Lord shall raise him up; and if he have committed sins, they shall be forgiven him. Confess your faults one to another, and pray one for another, that ye may be healed. The effectual fervent prayer of a righteous man availeth much. (James 5:15, 16).

"And whatsoever we ask, we receive of him, because we keep his commandments, and do those things that are pleasing in his sight" (1John 3:22).

"And this is the confidence that we have in him, that, if we ask any thing according to his will, he heareth us: and if we know that he hear us, whatsoever we ask, we know that we have the petitions that we desired of him. If any man see his brother sin a sin which is not unto death, he shall ask, and he shall give him life for them that sin not unto death" (1John 5:14-16).

7. Sanctifying Grace In General

"The LORD God is a sun and shield: the LORD will give grace and glory: no good thing will he withhold from them that walk uprightly" (Psalm 84:11).

"Sanctify them through thy truth: thy word is truth. And for their sakes I sanctify myself, that they also might be sanctified through the truth" (John 17:17, 19).

"We are his workmanship, created in Christ Jesus unto good works, which God hath before ordained that we should walk in them" (Ephesians 2:10).

"For it is God which worketh in you both to will and to do of his good pleasure" (Philippians 2:13).

"I can do all things through Christ which strengtheneth me" (Philippians 4:13).

"Not that we are sufficient of ourselves to think any thing as of ourselves; but our sufficiency is of God" (2Corinthians 3:5).

"And the very God of peace sanctify you wholly; and I pray God your whole spirit and soul and body be preserved blameless unto the coming of our Lord Jesus Christ" (1Thessalonians 5:23).

"Giving thanks unto the Father, which hath made us meet to be partakers of the inheritance of the saints in light. And you, that were sometime alienated and enemies in your mind by wicked works, yet now hath he reconciled in the body of his flesh through death, to present you holy and unblameable and unreproveable in his sight" (Colossians 1:12, 21, 22).

"We are bound to give thanks alway to God for you, brethren beloved of the Lord, because God hath from the beginning chosen you to salvation through sanctification of the Spirit and belief of the truth" (2Thessalonians 2:13).

"Who gave himself for us, that he might redeem us from all iniquity, and purify unto himself a peculiar people, zealous of good works" (Titus 2:14).

"This shall be the covenant that I will make with the house of Israel; after those days, saith the LORD, I will put my law in their inward parts, and write it in their hearts; and will be their God, and they shall be my people" (Jeremiah 31:33).

"That he would grant unto us, that we being delivered out of the hand of our enemies might serve him without fear, in holiness and righteousness before him, all the days of our life" (Luke 1:74, 75).

"They shall serve the LORD their God, and David their king, whom I will raise up unto them" (Jeremiah 30:9).

"And such were some of you: but ye are washed, but ye are sanctified, but ye are justified in the name of the Lord Jesus, and by the Spirit of our God" (1Corinthians 6:11).

"But we all, with open face beholding as in a glass the glory of the Lord, are changed into the same image from glory to glory, even as by the Spirit of the Lord" (2Corinthians 3:18).

8. Of Converting Grace

"And the LORD thy God will circumcise thine heart, and the heart of thy seed, to love the LORD thy God with all thine heart, and with all thy soul, that thou mayest live" (Deuteronomy 30:6).

"I will give them an heart to know me, that I am the LORD: and they shall be my people, and I will be their God: for they shall return unto me with their whole heart" (Jeremiah 24:7).

"Turn thou me, and I shall be turned; for thou art the LORD my God" (Jeremiah 31:18).

"Thy people shall be willing in the day of thy power" (Psalm 110:3).

"Not by works of righteousness which we have done, but

according to his mercy he saved us, by the washing of regeneration, and renewing of the Holy Ghost" (Titus 3:5).

"A new heart also will I give you, and a new spirit will I put within you: and I will take away the stony heart out of your flesh, and I will give you an heart of flesh" (Ezekiel 36:26).

"Who hath saved us, and called us with an holy calling, not according to our works, but according to his own purpose and grace, which was given us in Christ Jesus before the world began" (2Timothy 1:9).

"And I will give them one heart, and I will put a new spirit within you; and I will take the stony heart out of their flesh, and will give them an heart of flesh: That they may walk in my statutes, and keep mine ordinances, and do them: and they shall be my people, and I will be their God" (Ezekiel 11:19, 20).

"In those days, and in that time, saith the LORD, the children of Israel shall come, they and the children of Judah together, going and weeping: they shall go, and seek the LORD their God. They shall ask the way to Zion with their faces thitherward, saying, Come, and let us join ourselves to the LORD in a perpetual covenant that shall not be forgotten" (Jeremiah 50:4, 5).

The Grace Of Repentance

"They shall look upon me whom they have pierced" (Zechariah 12:10).

"Unto you first God, having raised up his Son Jesus, sent him to bless you, in turning away every one of you from his iniquities"

(Acts 3:26).

"Him hath God exalted with his right hand to be a Prince and a Saviour, for to give repentance to Israel, and forgiveness of sins" (Acts 5:31).

"Then shall ye remember your own evil ways, and your doings that were not good, and shall lothe yourselves in your own sight for your iniquities and for your abominations" (Ezekiel 36:31).

"Behold, I will hedge up thy way with thorns, and make a wall, that she shall not find her paths. And she shall follow after her lovers, but she shall not overtake them; and she shall seek them, but shall not find them: then shall she say, I will go and return to my first husband; for then was it better with me than now" (Hosea 2:6, 7).

"I am not come to call the righteous, but sinners to repentance" (Matthew 9:13).

"And there shall ye remember your ways, and all your doings, wherein ye have been defiled; and ye shall lothe yourselves in your own sight for all your evils that ye have committed" (Ezekiel 20:43).

The Grace Of Faith

"Unto you it is given in the behalf of Christ, not only to believe on him, but also to suffer for his sake" (Philippians 1:29).

"For by grace are ye saved through faith; and that not of yourselves: it is the gift of God" (Ephesians 2:8).

"It is written in the prophets, And they shall be all taught of God. Every man therefore that hath heard, and hath learned of the Father, cometh unto me" (John 6:45).

Grace To Fear God

"I will give them one heart, and one way, that they may fear me for ever" (Jeremiah 32:39).

9. Knowledge, Wisdom, Etc.

Knowledge

"Evil men understand not judgment: but they that seek the LORD understand all things" (Proverbs 28:5).

"He will teach us of his ways, and we will walk in his paths: for out of Zion shall go forth the law, and the word of the LORD from Jerusalem" (Isaiah 2:3).

"God, who commanded the light to shine out of darkness, hath shined in our hearts, to give the light of the knowledge of the glory of God in the face of Jesus Christ" (2Corinthians 4:6).

"Then shalt thou understand the fear of the LORD, and find the knowledge of God. Then shalt thou understand righteousness, and judgment, and equity; yea, every good path" (Proverbs 2:5, 9).

"And an highway shall be there, and a way, and it shall be called The way of holiness; the unclean shall not pass over it; but it shall be for those: the wayfaring men, though fools, shall not err therein" (Isaiah 35:8).

"And in that day shall the deaf hear the words of the book, and the eyes of the blind shall see out of obscurity, and out of darkness. They also that erred in spirit shall come to understanding, and they that murmured shall learn doctrine" (Isaiah 29:18, 24).

"Then shall we know, if we follow on to know the LORD" (Hosea 6:3).

"Therefore my people shall know my name: therefore they shall know in that day that I am he that doth speak" (Isaiah 52:6).

"I thank thee, O Father, Lord of heaven and earth, because thou hast hid these things from the wise and prudent, and hast revealed them unto babes" (Matthew 11:25).

"And we know that the Son of God is come, and hath given us an understanding, that we may know him that is true, and we are in him that is true, even in his Son Jesus Christ" (1John 5:20).

"And they shall teach no more every man his neighbour, and every man his brother, saying, Know the LORD: for they shall all know me, from the least of them unto the greatest of them, saith the LORD" (Jeremiah 31:34).

"To give knowledge of salvation unto his people by the remission of their sins, through the tender mercy of our God; whereby the dayspring from on high hath visited us, to give light to them that sit in darkness and in the shadow of death, to guide our feet into the way of peace" (Luke 1:77-79).

"He hath sent me to heal the brokenhearted, to preach deliverance to the captives, and recovering of sight to the blind" (Luke 4:18).

"And the eyes of them that see shall not be dim, and the ears of them that hear shall hearken" (Isaiah 32:3).

"To open the blind eyes, to bring out the prisoners from the prison, and them that sit in darkness out of the prison house" (Isaiah 42:7).

"Then spake Jesus again unto them, saying, I am the light of the world: he that followeth me shall not walk in darkness, but shall have the light of life" (John 8:12).

"The natural man receiveth not the things of the Spirit of God: for they are foolishness unto him: neither can he know them, because they are spiritually discerned. But he that is spiritual judgeth all things, yet he himself is judged of no man" (1Corinthians 2:14, 15).

Wisdom

"I will bless the LORD, who hath given me counsel: my reins also instruct me in the night seasons" (Psalm 16:7).

"The LORD giveth wisdom: out of his mouth cometh knowledge and understanding. He layeth up sound wisdom for the righteous" (Proverbs 2:6, 7).

"For God giveth to a man that is good in his sight wisdom, and knowledge" (Ecclesiastes 2:26).

"Behold, thou desirest truth in the inward parts: and in the hidden part thou shalt make me to know wisdom" (Psalm 51:6).

"If any of you lack wisdom, let him ask of God, that giveth to all men liberally, and upbraideth not; and it shall be given him" (James 1:5).

Divine Teaching

"I will instruct thee and teach thee in the way which thou shalt go: I will guide thee with mine eye" (Psalm 32:8).

"If any man will do his will, he shall know of the doctrine, whether it be of God, or whether I speak of myself" (John 7:17).

"Good and upright is the LORD: therefore will he teach sinners in the way. What man is he that feareth the LORD? him shall he teach in the way that he shall choose" (Psalm 25:8, 12).

Divine Guidance

"Thine ears shall hear a word behind thee, saying, This is the way, walk ye in it, when ye turn to the right hand, and when ye turn to the left" (Isaiah 30:21).

"I will direct their work in truth" (Isaiah 61:8).

"Thou shalt guide me with thy counsel" (Psalm 73:24).

"And the LORD shall guide thee continually" (Isaiah 58:11).

"He restoreth my soul: he leadeth me in the paths of righteousness for his name's sake" (Psalm 23:3).

"He that hath mercy on them shall lead them, even by the springs of water shall he guide them" (Isaiah 49:10).

"He led him about, he instructed him, he kept him as the apple of his eye. As an eagle stirreth up her nest, fluttereth over her young, spreadeth abroad her wings, taketh them, beareth them on her wings: so the LORD alone did lead him" (Deuteronomy 32:10-12).

Ability For Good Discourse

"The mouth of the just bringeth forth wisdom: but the froward tongue shall be cut out. The lips of the righteous know what is acceptable" (Proverbs 10:31, 32).

"The heart also of the rash shall understand knowledge, and the tongue of the stammerers shall be ready to speak plainly" (Isaiah 32:4).

"The preparations of the heart in man, and the answer of the tongue, is from the LORD" (Proverbs 16:1).

"To one is given by the Spirit the word of wisdom; to another the word of knowledge by the same Spirit" (1Corinthians 12:8).

"I will give you a mouth and wisdom, which all your adversaries shall not be able to gainsay nor resist" (Luke 21:15).

10. The Means Of Grace

"He maketh me to lie down in green pastures: he leadeth me beside the still waters" (Psalm 23:2).

"They shall feed in the ways, and their pastures shall be in all high places. They shall not hunger nor thirst; neither shall the heat nor sun smite them" (Isaiah 49:9, 10).

"How beautiful upon the mountains are the feet of him that bringeth good tidings, that publisheth peace; that bringeth good tidings of good, that publisheth salvation; that saith unto Zion, Thy God reigneth! Thy watchmen shall lift up the voice; with the voice together shall they sing: for they shall see eye to eye, when the LORD shall bring again Zion" (Isaiah 52:7, 8).

"I have set watchmen upon thy walls, O Jerusalem, which shall never hold their peace day nor night" (Isaiah 62:6).

"And I will give you pastors according to mine heart, which shall feed you with knowledge and understanding" (Jeremiah 3:15).

"I will open rivers in high places, and fountains in the midst of the valleys: I will make the wilderness a pool of water, and the dry land springs of water" (Isaiah 41:18).

"Their soul shall be as a watered garden; and they shall not sorrow any more at all. And I will satiate the soul of the priests with fatness, and my people shall be satisfied with my goodness, saith the LORD" (Jeremiah 31:12, 14).

"And though the Lord give you the bread of adversity, and the water of affliction, yet shall not thy teachers be removed into a corner any more, but thine eyes shall see thy teachers" (Isaiah 30:20).

"Them will I bring to my holy mountain, and make them joyful in my house of prayer: their burnt offerings and their sacrifices shall be accepted upon mine altar; for mine house shall be called an house of prayer for all people" (Isaiah 56:7).

"I will feed my flock, and I will cause them to lie down, saith the Lord GOD" (Ezekiel 34:15).

"He gave some, apostles; and some, prophets; and some, evangelists; and some, pastors and teachers; for the perfecting of the Saints, for the work of the ministry, for the edifying of the body of Christ: till we all come in the unity of the faith, and of the knowledge of the Son of God, unto a perfect man, unto the measure of the stature of the fulness of Christ" (Ephesians 4:11-13).

A Blessing Upon Ordinances

"They shall be abundantly satisfied with the fatness of thy house; and thou shalt make them drink of the river of thy pleasures. For with thee is the fountain of life: in thy light shall we see light" (Psalm 36:8, 9).

"To see thy power and thy glory, so as I have seen thee in the sanctuary. Because thy lovingkindness is better than life, my lips shall praise thee. Thus will I bless thee while I live: I will lift up my hands in thy name. My soul shall be satisfied as with marrow and fatness; and my mouth shall praise thee with joyful lips" (Psalm 63:2-5).

"I sat down under his shadow with great delight, and his fruit was sweet to my taste" (Song of Solomon 2:3).

"Those that be planted in the house of the LORD shall flourish in the courts of our God" (Psalm 92:13).

"They have seen thy goings, O God; even the goings of my God, my King, in the sanctuary" (Psalm 68:24).

"Blessed is the man whom thou choosest, and causest to approach unto thee, that he may dwell in thy courts: we shall be satisfied with the goodness of thy house, even of thy holy temple" (Psalm 65:4).

"Blessed is the people that know the joyful sound: they shall walk, O LORD, in the light of thy countenance. In thy name shall they rejoice all the day: and in thy righteousness shall they be exalted" (Psalm 89:15, 16).

"Blessed are they that dwell in thy house: they will be still praising thee. For a day in thy courts is better than a thousand. I had rather be a doorkeeper in the house of my God, than to dwell in the tents of wickedness. The LORD will give grace and glory" (Psalm 84:4, 11).

"I am the LORD thy God which teacheth thee to profit" (Isaiah 48:17).

"With joy shall ye draw water out of the wells of salvation" (Isaiah 12:3).

"They shall come up with acceptance on mine altar, and I will glorify the house of my glory" (Isaiah 60:7).

"Where two or three are gathered together in my name, there am I in the midst of them" (Matthew 18:20).

11. Of Grace Against Sin And Temptation

To Mortify Sin

"Ephraim shall say, What have I to do any more with idols?" (Hosea 14:8).

"O wretched man that I am! who shall deliver me from the body of this death? I thank God through Jesus Christ our Lord. So then with the mind I myself serve the law of God; but with the flesh the law of sin" (Romans 7:24, 25).

"Knowing this, that our old man is crucified with him, that the body of sin might be destroyed, that henceforth we should not serve sin. Sin shall not have dominion over you: for ye are not under the law, but under grace" (Romans 6:6, 14).

"Walk in the Spirit, and ye shall not fulfil the lust of the flesh" (Galatians 5:16).

"Ye shall know the truth, and the truth shall make you free [that is, from sin, ver. 34]" (John 8:32).

"Every branch that beareth fruit, he purgeth it, that it may bring forth more fruit" (John 15:2).

"The law of the Spirit of life in Christ Jesus hath made me free from the law of sin and death. For what the law could not do, in that it was weak through the flesh, God sending his own Son in the likeness of sinful flesh, and for sin, condemned sin in the flesh: that the righteousness of the law might be fulfilled in us, who walk not after the flesh, but after the Spirit" (Romans 8:2-4).

Against Temptation

"Nay, in all these things we are more than conquerors through him that loved us" (Romans 8:37).

"God is faithful, who will not suffer you to be tempted above that ye are able; but will with the temptation also make a way to escape, that ye may be able to bear it" (1Corinthians 10:13).

"He that feareth God shall come forth of them all" (Ecclesiastes 7:18).

"The Lord knoweth how to deliver the godly out of temptations" (2Peter 2:9).

"My grace is sufficient for thee: for my strength is made perfect in weakness" (2Corinthians 12:9).

"In that he himself hath suffered being tempted, he is able to succour them that are tempted" (Hebrews 2:18).

"Ye are of God, little children, and have overcome them: because greater is he that is in you, than he that is in the world" (1John 4:4).

From The Enticement Of Sinners

"To deliver thee from the way of the evil man, from the man that speaketh froward things; To deliver thee from the strange woman, even from the stranger which flattereth with her words" (Proverbs 2:12, 16).

"I find more bitter than death the woman, whose heart is snares and nets, and her hands as bands: whoso pleaseth God shall escape from her; but the sinner shall be taken by her" (Ecclesiastes 7:26).

Victory Over The World

"Be of good cheer; I have overcome the world" (John 16:33).

"By whom [Christ] the world is crucified unto me, and I unto the world" (Galatians 6:14).

"Who gave himself for our sins, that he might deliver us from this present evil world" (Galatians 1:4).

"I pray not that thou shouldest take them out of the world, but that thou shouldest keep them from the evil" (John 17:15).

"For whatsoever is born of God overcometh the world: and this is the victory that overcometh the world, even our faith. Who is he that overcometh the world, but he that believeth that Jesus is the Son of God?" (1John 5:4, 5).

Victory Over The Devil

"Resist the devil, and he will flee from you" (James 4:7).

"I will put enmity between thee and the woman, and between thy seed and her seed; it shall bruise thy head, and thou shalt bruise his heel" (Genesis 3:15).

"Simon, Simon, behold, Satan hath desired to have you, that he may sift you as wheat: But I have prayed for thee, that thy faith fail not" (Luke 22:31, 32).

"And the God of peace shall bruise Satan under your feet shortly" (Romans 16:20).

"I have written unto you, young men, because ye are strong, and the word of God abideth in you, and ye have overcome the wicked one" (1John 2:14).

"We know that whosoever is born of God sinneth not; but he that is begotten of God keepeth himself, and that wicked one toucheth him not" (1John 5:18).

12. Strength, Courage, And Resolution

"A bruised reed shall he not break, and the smoking flax shall he not quench: he shall bring forth judgment unto truth" (Isaiah 42:3).

"Behold, God is my salvation; I will trust, and not be afraid: for the LORD JEHOVAH is my strength and my song; he also is become my salvation" (Isaiah 12:2).

"He giveth power to the faint; and to them that have no might he increaseth strength. Even the youths shall faint and be weary, and the young men shall utterly fall: but they that wait upon the LORD shall renew their strength; they shall mount up with wings as eagles; they shall run, and not be weary; and they shall walk, and not faint" (Isaiah 40:29-31).

"Thou shalt be stedfast, and shalt not fear" (Job 11:15).

"My grace is sufficient for thee: for my strength is made perfect in weakness" (2Corinthians 12:9).

"Be of good courage, and he shall strengthen your heart, all ye that hope in the LORD" (Psalm 31:24).

"I will strengthen them in the LORD; and they shall walk up and down in his name, saith the LORD" (Zechariah 10:12).

"O God, thou art terrible out of thy holy places: the God of Israel is he that giveth strength and power unto his people" (Psalm 68:35).

"In that day shall the LORD defend the inhabitants of Jerusalem; and he that is feeble among them at that day shall be as David; and the house of David shall be as God, as the angel of the LORD before them" (Zechariah 12:8).

"Strengthen ye the weak hands, and confirm the feeble knees. Say to them that are of a fearful heart, Be strong, fear not: behold, your God will come with vengeance, even God with a recompence; he will come and save you" (Isaiah 35:3, 4).

"The LORD will be the hope of his people, and the strength of the children of Israel" (Joel 3:16).

"God hath not given us the spirit of fear; but of power, and of love, and of a sound mind" (2Timothy 1:7).

13. Fruitfulness And Increase Of Grace

Fruitfulness

"If these things be in you, and abound, they make you that ye shall neither be barren nor unfruitful in the knowledge of our Lord Jesus Christ" (2Peter 1:8).

"I will be as the dew unto Israel: he shall grow as the lily, and cast forth his roots as Lebanon. I am like a green fir tree. From me is thy fruit found" (Hosea 14:5, 8).

"He shall be like a tree planted by the rivers of water, that bringeth forth his fruit in his season; his leaf also shall not wither; and whatsoever he doeth shall prosper" (Psalm 1:3).

"They shall come and sing in the height of Zion, and shall flow together to the goodness of the LORD, for wheat, and for wine, and for oil, and for the young of the flock and of the herd: and their soul shall be as a watered garden; and they shall not sorrow any more at all" (Jeremiah 31:12).

"Every branch that beareth fruit, he purgeth it, that it may bring forth more fruit. He that abideth in me, and I in him, the same bringeth forth much fruit: for without me ye can do nothing" (John 15:2, 5).

In Old Age

"They shall still bring forth fruit in old age; they shall be fat and flourishing" (Psalm 92:14).

Increase In Grace

"The righteous also shall hold on his way, and he that hath clean hands shall be stronger and stronger" (Job 17:9).

"They go from strength to strength, every one of them in Zion appeareth before God" (Psalm 84:7).

"The righteous shall flourish like the palm tree: he shall grow like a cedar in Lebanon" (Psalm 92:12).

"The path of the just is as the shining light, that shineth more and more unto the perfect day" (Proverbs 4:18).

"But unto you that fear my name shall the Sun of righteousness arise with healing in his wings; and ye shall go forth, and grow up as calves of the stall" (Malachi 4:2).

"Whosoever hath, to him shall be given, and he shall have more abundance" (Matthew 13:12).

"But he giveth more grace. Wherefore he saith, God resisteth the proud, but giveth grace unto the humble" (James 4:6).

The Grace Of Meekness

"The wolf also shall dwell with the lamb, and the leopard shall lie down with the kid; and the calf and the young lion and the fatling together; and a little child shall lead them. And the cow and the bear shall feed; their young ones shall lie down together:

and the lion shall eat straw like the ox. And the sucking child shall play on the hole of the asp, and the weaned child shall put his hand on the cockatrice' den. They shall not hurt nor destroy in all my holy mountain: for the earth shall be full of the knowledge of the LORD, as the waters cover the sea" (Isaiah 11:6-9).

14. Grace To Persevere

"And I give unto them eternal life; and they shall never perish, neither shall any man pluck them out of my hand. My Father, which gave them me, is greater than all; and no man is able to pluck them out of my Father's hand" (John 10:28, 29).

"The Lord is faithful, who shall stablish you, and keep you from evil" (2Thessalonians 3:3).

"He which stablisheth us with you in Christ, and hath anointed us, is God" (2Corinthians 1:21).

"Who shall also confirm you unto the end, that ye may be blameless in the day of our Lord Jesus Christ" (1Corinthians 1:8).

"Holy Father, keep through thine own name those whom thou hast given me, that they may be one, as we are" (John 17:11).

"Being confident of this very thing, that he which hath begun a good work in you will perform it until the day of Jesus Christ" (Philippians 1:6).

"I pray God your whole spirit and soul and body be preserved blameless unto the coming of our Lord Jesus Christ. Faithful is he that calleth you, who also will do it" (1Thessalonians 5:23, 24).

"I am persuaded, that neither death, nor life, nor angels, nor principalities, nor powers, nor things present, nor things to come, nor height, nor depth, nor any other creature, shall be able to separate us from the love of God, which is in Christ Jesus our Lord" (Romans 8:38, 39).

"The righteous is an everlasting foundation" (Proverbs 10:25).

"When I said, My foot slippeth; thy mercy, O LORD, held me up" (Psalm 94:18).

"Who are kept by the power of God through faith unto salvation" (1Peter 1:5).

"Unto him that is able to keep you from falling, and to present you faultless before the presence of his glory with exceeding joy" (Jude 24).

"Wherefore the rather, brethren, give diligence to make your calling and election sure: for if ye do these things, ye shall never fall" (2Peter 1:10).

"The LORD will perfect that which concerneth me: thy mercy, O LORD, endureth for ever: forsake not the works of thine own hands" (Psalm 138:8).

"We know that whosoever is born of God sinneth not; but he that is begotten of God keepeth himself, and that wicked one toucheth him not" (1John 5:18).

15. Sanctified Afflictions

"Happy is the man whom God correcteth: therefore despise not thou the chastening of the Almighty: For he maketh sore, and bindeth up: he woundeth, and his hands make whole" (Job 5:17, 18).

"As a man chasteneth his son, so the LORD thy God chasteneth thee" (Deuteronomy 8:5).

"Whom the LORD loveth he correcteth; even as a father the son in whom he delighteth" (Proverbs 3:12).

"I will turn my hand upon thee, and purely purge away thy dross, and take away all thy tin" (Isaiah 1:25).

"Blessed is the man whom thou chastenest, O LORD, and teachest him out of thy law; that thou mayest give him rest from the days of adversity, until the pit be digged for the wicked" (Psalm 94:12, 13).

"Before I was afflicted I went astray: but now have I kept thy word. It is good for me that I have been afflicted; that I might learn thy statutes. I know, O LORD, that thy judgments are right, and that thou in faithfulness hast afflicted me" (Psalm 119:67, 71, 75).

"And if they be bound in fetters, and be holden in cords of affliction; then he sheweth them their work, and their transgressions that they have exceeded. He openeth also their ear to discipline, and commandeth that they return from iniquity" (Job 36:8-10).

"Behold, I have refined thee, but not with silver; I have chosen thee in the furnace of affliction" (Isaiah 48:10).

"By this therefore shall the iniquity of Jacob be purged; and this is all the fruit to take away his sin" (Isaiah 27:9).

"When we are judged, we are chastened of the Lord, that we should not be condemned with the world" (1Corinthians 11:32).

"We glory in tribulations also: knowing that tribulation worketh patience; and patience, experience; and experience, hope" (Romans 5:3, 4).

"For which cause we faint not; but though our outward man perish, yet the inward man is renewed day by day. For our light affliction, which is but for a moment, worketh for us a far more exceeding and eternal weight of glory" (2Corinthians 4:16, 17).

"I will hedge up thy way with thorns, and make a wall, that she shall not find her paths. And she shall follow after her lovers, but she shall not overtake them; and she shall seek them, but shall not find them: then shall she say, I will go and return to my first husband; for then was it better with me than now" (Hosea 2:6, 7).

"As many as I love, I rebuke and chasten" (Revelation 3:19).

"I know that this shall turn to my salvation through your prayer, and the supply of the Spirit of Jesus Christ" (Philippians 1:19).

"Some of them of understanding shall fall, to try them, and to purge, and to make them white, even to the time of the end" (Daniel 11:35).

"The trying of your faith worketh patience. Blessed is the man that endureth temptation: for when he is tried, he shall receive the crown of life, which the Lord hath promised to them that love him" (James 1:3, 12).

"Whom the Lord loveth he chasteneth, and scourgeth every son whom he receiveth. If ye endure chastening, God dealeth with you as with sons; for what son is he whom the father chasteneth not? They verily for a few days chastened us after their own pleasure; but he for our profit, that we might be partakers of his holiness. Now no chastening for the present seemeth to be joyous, but grievous: nevertheless afterward it yieldeth the peaceable fruit of righteousness unto them which are exercised thereby" (Hebrews 12:6, 7, 10, 11).

"Many shall be purified, and made white, and tried" (Daniel 12:10).

"That the trial of your faith, being much more precious than of gold that perisheth, though it be tried with fire, might be found unto praise and honour and glory at the appearing of Jesus Christ" (1Peter 1:7).

"I will bring the third part through the fire, and will refine them as silver is refined, and will try them as gold is tried: they shall call on my name, and I will hear them: I will say, It is my people: and they shall say, The LORD is my God" (Zechariah 13:9).

16. Grace To The Children Of Israel

"And the LORD thy God will circumcise thine heart, and the heart of thy seed, to love the LORD thy God with all thine heart, and with all thy soul, that thou mayest live" (Deuteronomy 30:6).

"I will establish my covenant between me and thee and thy seed after thee in their generations for an everlasting covenant, to be a God unto thee, and to thy seed after thee. Thou shalt keep my covenant therefore, thou, and thy seed after thee in their generations" (Genesis 17:7, 9).

"Now are they [your children] holy" (1Corinthians 7:14).

"The promise is unto you, and to your children" (Acts 2:39).

"Believe on the Lord Jesus Christ, and thou shalt be saved, and thy house" (Acts 16:31).

"All thy children shall be taught of the LORD; and great shall be the peace of thy children" (Isaiah 54:13).

"Suffer the little children to come unto me, and forbid them not: for of such is the kingdom of God. And he took them up in his arms, put his hands upon them, and blessed them" (Mark 10:14, 16).

"I will pour my Spirit upon thy seed, and my blessing upon thine offspring: and they shall spring up as among the grass, as willows by the water courses. One shall say, I am the LORD'S; and another shall call himself by the name of Jacob; and another shall subscribe with his hand unto the LORD, and surname himself by the name of Israel" (Isaiah 44:3-5).

17. An Interest In God

As Our God

"I will establish my covenant between me and thee and thy seed after thee in their generations for an everlasting covenant, to be a God unto thee" (Genesis 17:7).

"God himself shall be with them, and be their God" (Revelation 21:3).

"Ye shall be my people, and I will be your God" (Jeremiah 30:22).

"I will be their God, and they shall be my people" (2Corinthians 6:16).

"I will be to them a God, and they shall be to me a people" (Hebrews 8:10).

"And I will walk among you, and will be your God, and ye shall be my people" (Leviticus 26:12).

"This God is our God for ever and ever: he will be our guide even unto death" (Psalm 48:14).

"Fear thou not; for I am with thee: be not dismayed; for I am thy God" (Isaiah 41:10).

"For thy Maker is thine husband; the LORD of hosts is his name; and thy Redeemer the Holy One of Israel; The God of the whole earth shall he be called" (Isaiah 54:5).

"I the LORD will be their God, and my servant David a prince among them. Ye my flock, the flock of my pasture, are men, and I am your God, saith the Lord GOD" (Ezekiel 34:24, 31).

"God is not ashamed to be called their God: for he hath prepared for them a city" (Hebrews 11:16).

Our Portion

"I am thy shield, and thy exceeding great reward" (Genesis 15:1).

"The LORD is the portion of mine inheritance and of my cup" (Psalm 16:5).

"The LORD is my portion, saith my soul; therefore will I hope in him" (Lamentations 3:24).

"My flesh and my heart faileth: but God is the strength of my heart, and my portion for ever" (Psalm 73:26).

Our Glory

"In that day shall the LORD of hosts be for a crown of glory, and for a diadem of beauty, unto the residue of his people" (Isaiah 28:5).

His Presence With Us

"The upright shall dwell in thy presence" (Psalm 140:13).

"My presence shall go with thee, and I will give thee rest" (Exodus 33:14).

"The LORD his God is with him, and the shout of a king is among them" (Numbers 23:21).

"Fear thou not; for I am with thee" (Isaiah 41:10).

"Thus shall they know that I the LORD their God am with them" (Ezekiel 34:30).

"The LORD is with you, while ye be with him; and if ye seek him, he will be found of you" (2Chronicles 15:2).

"The LORD, he it is that doth go before thee; he will be with thee, he will not fail thee, neither forsake thee" (Deuteronomy 31:8).

"If a man love me, he will keep my words: and my Father will love him, and we will come unto him, and make our abode with him" (John 14:23).

"And ye shall know that I am in the midst of Israel, and that I am the LORD your God, and none else: and my people shall never be ashamed" (Joel 2:27).

His Love

"The LORD hath set apart him that is godly for himself" (Psalm 4:3).

"He will love thee, and bless thee, and multiply thee" (Deuteronomy 7:13).

"The LORD will command his lovingkindness in the daytime" (Psalm 42:8).

"The LORD loveth the righteous" (Psalm 146:8).

"I will heal their backsliding, I will love them freely" (Hosea 14:4).

"He loveth him that followeth after righteousness" (Proverbs 15:9).

"Thou shalt be called Hephzibah, and thy land Beulah: for the LORD delighteth in thee" (Isaiah 62:4).

"As the bridegroom rejoiceth over the bride, so shall thy God rejoice over thee" (Isaiah 62:5).

"Since thou wast precious in my sight, thou hast been honourable, and I have loved thee" (Isaiah 43:4).

"I have loved thee with an everlasting love: therefore with lovingkindness have I drawn thee" (Jeremiah 31:3).

"I will rejoice over them to do them good, and I will plant them in this land assuredly with my whole heart and with my whole soul" (Jeremiah 32:41).

"The LORD thy God in the midst of thee is mighty; he will save, he will rejoice over thee with joy; he will rest in his love, he will joy over thee with singing" (Zephaniah 3:17).

"For his great love wherewith he loved us" (Ephesians 2:4).

"I will call them my people, which were not my people; and her beloved, which was not beloved" (Romans 9:25).

"Who crowneth thee with lovingkindness and tender mercies" (Psalm 103:4).

"For the Father himself loveth you, because ye have loved me" (John 16:27).

"Now our Lord Jesus Christ himself, and God, even our Father, which hath loved us" (2Thessalonians 2:16).

"That the world may know that thou hast sent me, and hast loved them, as thou hast loved me. That the love wherewith thou hast loved me may be in them, and I in them" (John 17:23, 26).

"Herein is love, not that we loved God, but that he loved us. and sent his Son to be the propitiation for our sins. We have known and believed the love that God hath to us. God is love; and he that dwelleth in love dwelleth in God, and God in him. We love him, because he first loved us" (1John 4:10, 16, 19).

His Mercy

"In my wrath I smote thee, but in my favour have I had mercy on thee" (Isaiah 60:10).

"The LORD thy God is a merciful God; he will not forsake thee, neither destroy thee" (Deuteronomy 4:31).

"My bowels are troubled for him; I will surely have mercy upon him" (Jeremiah 31:20).

"I will sow her unto me in the earth; and I will have mercy upon her that had not obtained mercy" (Hosea 2:23).

"For my name's sake will I defer mine anger, and for my praise will I refrain for thee, that I cut thee not off" (Isaiah 48:9).

"Therefore will the LORD wait, that he may be gracious unto you, and therefore will he be exalted, that he may have mercy upon you" (Isaiah 30:18).

"Like as a father pitieth his children, so the LORD pitieth them that fear him. The mercy of the LORD is from everlasting to everlasting upon them that fear him" (Psalm 103:13, 17).

"How shall I give thee up, Ephraim? how shall I deliver thee, Israel? how shall I make thee as Admah? how shall I set thee as Zeboim? mine heart is turned within me, my repentings are kindled together. I will not execute the fierceness of mine anger, I will not return to destroy Ephraim" (Hosea 11:8, 9).

"God exacteth of thee less than thine iniquity deserveth" (Job 11:6).

"I will make all my goodness pass before thee, and I will proclaim the name of the LORD before thee; and will be gracious to whom I will be gracious, and will shew mercy on whom I will shew mercy" (Exodus 33:19).

His Help

"The God of Jacob is our refuge. Selah" (Psalm 46:11).

"If God be for us, who can be against us?" (Romans 8:31).

"O Israel, thou hast destroyed thyself; but in me is thine help" (Hosea 13:9).

"Thou art my help and my deliverer; make no tarrying, O my God" (Psalm 40:17).

"The eternal God is thy refuge, and underneath are the everlasting arms: and he shall thrust out the enemy from before thee; and shall say, Destroy them. Happy art thou, O Israel: who is like unto thee, O people saved by the LORD, the shield of thy help, and who is the sword of thy excellency! and thine enemies shall be found liars unto thee; and thou shalt tread upon their high places" (Deuteronomy 33:27, 29).

"We may boldly say, The Lord is my helper, and I will not fear what man shall do unto me" (Hebrews 13:6).

"I will strengthen thee; yea, I will help thee; yea, I will uphold thee with the right hand of my righteousness. I the LORD thy God will hold thy right hand, saying unto thee, Fear not; I will help thee. Fear not, thou worm Jacob, and ye men of Israel; I will help thee, saith the LORD, and thy redeemer, the Holy One of Israel" (Isaiah 41:10, 13, 14).

His Care

"He that toucheth you toucheth the apple of his eye" (Zechariah 2:8).

"Casting all your care upon him; for he careth for you" (1Peter 5:7).

"The eye of the LORD is upon them that fear him, upon them that hope in his mercy" (Psalm 33:18).

"Hearken unto me, O house of Jacob, and all the remnant of the house of Israel, which are borne by me from the belly, which are carried from the womb: and even to your old age I am he; and even to hoar hairs will I carry you: I have made, and I will bear; even I will carry, and will deliver you" (Isaiah 46:3, 4).

"There shall not an hair of your head perish" (Luke 21:18).

"The very hairs of your head are all numbered" (Matthew 10:30).

"In all their affliction he was afflicted, and the Angel of his presence saved them: in his love and in his pity he redeemed them; and he bare them, and carried them all the days of old" (Isaiah 63:9).

"As an eagle stirreth up her nest, fluttereth over her young, spreadeth abroad her wings, taketh them, beareth them on her wings: so the LORD alone did lead him, and there was no strange god with him" (Deuteronomy 32:11, 12).

His Covenant With His People

"I will make an everlasting covenant with you, even the sure mercies of David" (Isaiah 55:3).

"He hath made with me an everlasting covenant, ordered in all things, and sure: for this is all my salvation, and all my desire" (2Samuel 23:5).

"I will betroth thee unto me for ever; yea, I will betroth thee unto me in righteousness, and in judgment, and in lovingkindness, and in mercies. I will even betroth thee unto me in faithfulness: and thou shalt know the LORD" (Hosea 2:19, 20).

God Will Not Forsake Them

"O Israel, thou shalt not be forgotten of me" (Isaiah 44:21).

"I will set my tabernacle among you: and my soul shall not abhor you" (Leviticus 26:11).

"The LORD will not cast off his people, neither will he forsake his inheritance" (Psalm 94:14).

"Zion said, The LORD hath forsaken me, and my Lord hath forgotten me. Can a woman forget her sucking child, that she should not have compassion on the son of her womb? yea, they may forget, yet will I not forget thee. Behold, I have graven thee upon the palms of my hands; thy walls are continually before me" (Isaiah 49:14-16).

"As I have sworn that the waters of Noah should no more go

over the earth; so have I sworn that I would not be wroth with thee, nor rebuke thee. For the mountains shall depart, and the hills be removed; but my kindness shall not depart from thee, neither shall the covenant of my peace be removed, saith the LORD that hath mercy on thee" (Isaiah 54:9, 10).

"I will never leave thee, nor forsake thee" (Hebrews 13:5).

"Thou, LORD, hast not forsaken them that seek thee" (Psalm 9:10).

"These things will I do unto them, and not forsake them" (Isaiah 42:16).

"For the LORD loveth judgment, and forsaketh not his saints; they are preserved for ever" (Psalm 37:28).

"The Lord will not cast off for ever: But though he cause grief, yet will he have compassion according to the multitude of his mercies" (Lamentations 3:31, 32).

"I will make an everlasting covenant with them, that I will not turn away from them, to do them good; but I will put my fear in their hearts, that they shall not depart from me" (Jeremiah 32:40).

18. An Interest In Christ

"Behold, I have given him for a witness to the people, a leader and commander to the people" (Isaiah 55:4).

"For unto us a child is born, unto us a son is given: and the government shall be upon his shoulder: and his name shall be called Wonderful, Counsellor, The mighty God, The everlasting Father, The Prince of Peace" (Isaiah 9:6).

"My beloved is mine, and I am his" (Song of Solomon 2:16).

"All that the Father giveth me shall come to me; and him that cometh to me I will in no wise cast out" (John 6:37).

"God so loved the world, that he gave his only begotten Son, that whosoever believeth in him should not perish, but have everlasting life" (John 3:16).

"I will set up one shepherd over them, and he shall feed them, even my servant David; he shall feed them, and he shall be their shepherd" (Ezekiel 34:23).

"But unto you that fear my name shall the Sun of righteousness arise with healing in his wings; and ye shall go forth, and grow up as calves of the stall" (Malachi 4:2).

"I the LORD have called thee in righteousness, and will hold thine hand, and will keep thee, and give thee for a covenant of the people, for a light of the Gentiles" (Isaiah 42:6).

All Grace From Christ

"Of his fulness have all we received, and grace for grace. For the law was given by Moses, but grace and truth came by Jesus Christ" (John 1:16, 17).

"The fulness of him that filleth all in all" (Ephesians 1:23).

"Surely, shall one say, in the LORD have I righteousness and strength" (Isaiah 45:24).

"Of him are ye in Christ Jesus, who of God is made unto us wisdom, and righteousness, and sanctification, and redemption" (1Corinthians 1:30).

"Him hath God exalted with his right hand to be a Prince and a Saviour, for to give repentance to Israel, and forgiveness of sins" (Acts 5:31).

Redemption By Christ

"That thou mayest say to the prisoners, Go forth; to them that are in darkness, Shew yourselves" (Isaiah 49:9).

"To open the blind eyes, to bring out the prisoners from the prison, and them that sit in darkness out of the prison house" (Isaiah 42:7).

"Ye know that ye were not redeemed with corruptible things, as silver and gold, from your vain conversation received by tradition from your fathers; but with the precious blood of Christ, as of a lamb without blemish and without spot" (1Peter 1:18, 19).

"The Son of man came not to be ministered unto, but to minister, and to give his life a ransom for many" (Mark 10:45).

"Christ hath redeemed us from the curse of the law, being made a curse for us" (Galatians 3:13).

"In whom we have redemption through his blood, the forgiveness of sins, according to the riches of his grace" (Ephesians 1:7).

"Walk in love, as Christ also hath loved us, and hath given himself for us an offering and a sacrifice to God for a sweetsmelling savour" (Ephesians 5:2).

"When the fulness of the time was come, God sent forth his Son, made of a woman, made under the law, to redeem them that were under the law, that we might receive the adoption of sons" (Galatians 4:4, 5).

"How much more shall the blood of Christ, who through the eternal Spirit offered himself without spot to God, purge your conscience from dead works to serve the living God? And for this cause he is the Mediator of the new testament, that by means of death, for the redemption of the transgressions that were under the first testament, they which are called might receive the promise of eternal inheritance" (Hebrews 9:14, 15).

"Christ our passover is sacrificed for us" (1Corinthians 5:7).

"Thou wast slain, and hast redeemed us to God by thy blood" (Revelation 5:9).

Life From Him

"Because I live, ye shall live also" (John 14:19).

"He that eateth me, even he shall live by me" (John 6:57).

"For ye are dead, and your life is hid with Christ in God. When Christ, who is our life, shall appear, then shall ye also appear with him in glory" (Colossians 3:3, 4).

"I am crucified with Christ: nevertheless I live; yet not I, but Christ liveth in me: and the life which I now live in the flesh I live by the faith of the Son of God, who loved me, and gave himself for me" (Galatians 2:20).

"You hath he quickened, who were dead in trespasses and sins; God, who is rich in mercy... even when we were dead in sins, hath quickened us together with Christ, (by grace ye are saved;) and hath raised us up together, and made us sit together in heavenly places in Christ Jesus" (Ephesians 2:1, 5, 6).

"He that hath the Son hath life" (1John 5:12).

"I am come that they might have life, and that they might have it more abundantly" (John 10:10).

"As the Father raiseth up the dead, and quickeneth them; even so the Son quickeneth whom he will" (John 5:21).

"Though he was crucified through weakness, yet he liveth by the power of God. For we also are weak in him, but we shall live with him by the power of God toward you" (2Corinthians 13:4).

"If we be dead with Christ, we believe that we shall also live with him: Reckon ye also yourselves to be dead indeed unto sin, but alive unto God through Jesus Christ our Lord" (Romans 6:8, 11).

His Intercession

"He bare the sin of many, and made intercession for the transgressors" (Isaiah 53:12).

"Wherefore he is able also to save them to the uttermost that come unto God by him, seeing he ever liveth to make intercession for them" (Hebrews 7:25).

"It is Christ... who also maketh intercession for us" (Romans 8:34).

"Christ is not entered into the holy places made with hands, which are the figures of the true; but into heaven itself, now to appear in the presence of God for us" (Hebrews 9:24).

"Seeing then that we have a great high priest, that is passed into the heavens, Jesus the Son of God, let us hold fast our profession. For we have not an high priest which cannot be touched with the feeling of our infirmities; but was in all points tempted like as we are, yet without sin. Let us therefore come boldly unto the throne of grace, that we may obtain mercy, and find grace to help in time of need" (Hebrews 4:14-16).

His Love

"As the Father hath loved me, so have I loved you: continue ye in my love" (John 15:9).

"Having loved his own which were in the world, he loved them unto the end. A new commandment I give unto you, That ye love one another; as I have loved you, that ye also love one another" (John 13:1, 34).

"And to know that I have loved thee" (Revelation 3:9).

"So shall the king greatly desire thy beauty" (Psalm 45:11).

"Christ also hath loved us, and hath given himself for us" (Ephesians 5:2).

"I am my beloved's, and his desire is toward me" (Song of Solomon 7:10).

"Thou hast ravished my heart, my sister, my spouse" (Song of Solomon 4:9).

"Unto him that loved us, and washed us from our sins in his own blood" (Revelation 1:5).

"In all these things we are more than conquerors through him that loved us" (Romans 8:37).

"His banner over me was love. His left hand is under my head, and his right hand doth embrace me" (Song of Solomon 2:4, 6).

His Care Of His Church

"Who walketh in the midst of the seven golden candlesticks" (Revelation 2:1).

"He shall feed his flock like a shepherd: he shall gather the lambs with his arm, and carry them in his bosom, and shall gently lead those that are with young" (Isaiah 40:11).

"A bruised reed shall he not break, and the smoking flax shall he not quench: he shall bring forth judgment unto truth" (Isaiah 42:3).

"Christ also loved the church, and gave himself for it; That he might sanctify and cleanse it with the washing of water by the word, That he might present it to himself a glorious church, not having spot, or wrinkle, or any such thing; but that it should be holy and without blemish. For no man ever yet hated his own flesh; but nourisheth and cherisheth it, even as the Lord the church" (Ephesians 5:25-27, 29).

His Presence With His People

"And truly our fellowship is with the Father, and with his Son Jesus Christ" (1John 1:3).

"I will not leave you comfortless: I will come to you. I will love him, and will manifest myself to him" (John 14:18, 21).

"Behold, I stand at the door, and knock: if any man hear my voice, and open the door, I will come in to him, and will sup with him, and he with me" (Revelation 3:20).

19. Promises Of The Spirit

"Behold, I will pour out my Spirit unto you, I will make known my words unto you" (Proverbs 1:23).

"Until the Spirit be poured upon us from on high, and the wilderness be a fruitful field" (Isaiah 32:15).

"And I will put my Spirit within you, and cause you to walk in my statutes, and ye shall keep my judgments, and do them" (Ezekiel 36:27).

"If ye then, being evil, know how to give good gifts unto your children: how much more shall your heavenly Father give the Holy Spirit to them that ask him?" (Luke 11:13).

"This is my covenant with them, saith the LORD; My Spirit that is upon thee, and my words which I have put in thy mouth, shall not depart out of thy mouth, nor out of the mouth of thy seed, nor out of the mouth of thy seed's seed, saith the LORD, from henceforth and for ever" (Isaiah 59:21).

"Jesus answered and said unto her, If thou knewest the gift of God, and who it is that saith to thee, Give me to drink; thou wouldest have asked of him, and he would have given thee living water. Whosoever drinketh of the water that I shall give him shall never thirst; but the water that I shall give him shall be in him a well of water springing up into everlasting life" (John 4:10, 14).

"The Holy Ghost which dwelleth in us" (2Timothy 1:14).

"That we might receive the promise of the Spirit through faith" (Galatians 3:14).

"Now we have received, not the spirit of the world, but the Spirit which is of God; that we might know the things that are freely given to us of God" (1Corinthians 2:12).

"He that believeth on me, as the Scripture hath said, out of his belly shall flow rivers of living water. But this spake he of the Spirit, which they that believe on him should receive: for the Holy Ghost was not yet given; because that Jesus was not yet glorified" (John 7:38, 39).

"I will pray the Father, and he shall give you another Comforter, that he may abide with you for ever; even the Spirit of truth; whom the world cannot receive, because it seeth him not, neither knoweth him: but ye know him; for he dwelleth with you, and shall be in you" (John 14:16, 17).

His Teaching

"The Holy Ghost shall teach you in the same hour what ye ought to say" (Luke 12:12).

"God hath revealed them unto us by his Spirit: for the Spirit searcheth all things, yea, the deep things of God" (1Corinthians 2:10).

"When he, the Spirit of truth, is come, he will guide you into all truth" (John 16:13).

"But the anointing which ye have received of him abideth in you, and ye need not that any man teach you: but as the same anointing teacheth you of all things, and is truth, and is no lie, and even as it hath taught you, ye shall abide in him" (1John 2:27).

Help In Prayer

"And because ye are sons, God hath sent forth the Spirit of his Son into your hearts, crying, Abba, Father" (Galatians 4:6).

"I will pour upon the house of David, and upon the inhabitants of Jerusalem, the spirit of grace and of supplications" (Zechariah 12:10).

"Ye have received the Spirit of adoption, whereby we cry, Abba, Father. The Spirit also helpeth our infirmities: for we know not what we should pray for as we ought: but the Spirit itself maketh intercession for us with groanings which cannot be uttered. And he that searcheth the hearts knoweth what is the mind of the

Spirit, because he maketh intercession for the saints according to the will of God" (Romans 8:15, 26, 27).

"LORD, thou hast heard the desire of the humble: thou wilt prepare their heart, thou wilt cause thine ear to hear" (Psalm 10:17).

To Witness Our Adoption

"The Spirit itself beareth witness with our spirit, that we are the children of God" (Romans 8:16).

To Seal Our Redemption

"Who hath also sealed us, and given the earnest of the Spirit in our hearts" (2Corinthians 1:22).

"Grieve not the Holy Spirit of God, whereby ye are sealed unto the day of redemption" (Ephesians 4:30).

"Now he that hath wrought us for the selfsame thing is God, who also hath given unto us the earnest of the Spirit" (2Corinthians 5:5).

"And hope maketh not ashamed; because the love of God is shed abroad in our hearts by the Holy Ghost which is given unto us" (Romans 5:5).

"After that ye believed, ye were sealed with that Holy Spirit of promise, Which is the earnest of our inheritance until the redemption of the purchased possession, unto the praise of his glory" (Ephesians 1:13, 14).

To Be Our Comforter

"He shall give you another Comforter, that he may abide with you for ever; I will not leave you comfortless: I will come to you" (John 14:16, 18).

"Then had the churches rest throughout all Judaea and Galilee and Samaria, and were edified; and walking in the fear of the Lord, and in the comfort of the Holy Ghost, were multiplied" (Acts 9:31).

THE JOYS OF THE HOLY GHOST

"The kingdom of God is not meat and drink; but righteousness, and peace, and joy in the Holy Ghost" (Romans 14:17).

20. The Ministry Of Angels

"The angel of the LORD encampeth round about them that fear him, and delivereth them" (Psalm 34:7).

"Are they not all ministering spirits, sent forth to minister for them who shall be heirs of salvation?" (Hebrews 1:14).

"He shall give his angels charge over thee, to keep thee in all thy ways. They shall bear thee up in their hands, lest thou dash thy foot against a stone" (Psalm 91:11, 12).

"Take heed that ye despise not one of these little ones; for I say unto you, That in heaven their angels do always behold the face of my Father which is in heaven" (Matthew 18:10).

21. That We Shall Be Kings And Priests Unto God

"And hath made us kings and priests unto God and his Father" (Revelation 1:6).

"Ye shall be unto me a kingdom of priests, and an holy nation" (Exodus 19:6).

"And hast made us unto our God kings and priests: and we shall reign on the earth" (Revelation 5:10).

"Ye are a chosen generation, a royal priesthood, an holy nation, a peculiar people; that ye should shew forth the praises of him who hath called you out of darkness into his marvellous light" (1Peter 2:9).

22. Peace Of Conscience, Comfort, And Hope

Peace Of Conscience

"The work of righteousness shall be peace; and the effect of righteousness quietness and assurance for ever" (Isaiah 32:17).

"His soul shall dwell at ease" (Psalm 25:13).

"Thy faith hath saved thee; go in peace" (Luke 7:50).

He will speak peace unto his people, and to his saints" (Psalm 85:8).

"He healeth the broken in heart, and bindeth up their wounds" (Psalm 147:3).

"Now the Lord of peace himself give you peace always by all means" (2Thessalonians 3:16).

"Let the peace of God rule in your hearts, to the which also ye are called in one body" (Colossians 3:15).

"Peace I leave with you, my peace I give unto you: not as the world giveth, give I unto you" (John 14:27).

"I create the fruit of the lips; Peace, peace to him that is far off, and to him that is near, saith the LORD" (Isaiah 57:19).

"The peace of God, which passeth all understanding, shall keep your hearts and minds through Christ Jesus" (Philippians 4:7).

Comfort

"And in that day thou shalt say, O LORD, I will praise thee: though thou wast angry with me, thine anger is turned away, and thou comfortedst me" (Isaiah 12:1).

"I will not leave you comfortless: I will come to you" (John 14:18).

"The LORD hath comforted his people, and will have mercy upon his afflicted" (Isaiah 49:13).

"I have seen his ways, and will heal him: I will lead him also, and restore comforts unto him and to his mourners" (Isaiah 57:18).

"Stand ye in the ways, and see, and ask for the old paths, where is the good way, and walk therein, and ye shall find rest for your souls" (Jeremiah 6:16).

"For a small moment have I forsaken thee; but with great mercies will I gather thee. In a little wrath I hid my face from thee for a moment; but with everlasting kindness will I have mercy on thee, saith the LORD thy Redeemer" (Isaiah 54:7, 8).

"He hath sent me to bind up the brokenhearted, to proclaim liberty to the captives, and the opening of the prison to them that are bound; to proclaim the acceptable year of the LORD, and the day of vengeance of our God; to comfort all that mourn; to appoint unto them that mourn in Zion, to give unto them beauty for ashes, the oil of joy for mourning, the garment of praise for the spirit of heaviness; that they might be called trees of righteousness, the planting of the LORD, that he might be glorified" (Isaiah 61:1-3).

"I, even I, am he that comforteth you:" (Isaiah 51:12).

"A good man shall be satisfied from himself" (Proverbs 14:14).

"God, that comforteth those that are cast down, comforted us by the coming of Titus" (2Corinthians 7:6).

"Now our Lord Jesus Christ himself, and God, even our Father, which hath loved us, and hath given us everlasting consolation and good hope through grace, comfort your hearts" (2Thessalonians 2:16, 17).

"That ye may suck, and be satisfied with the breasts of her consolations; that ye may milk out, and be delighted with the abundance of her glory. As one whom his mother comforteth, so will I comfort you; and ye shall be comforted in Jerusalem" (Isaiah 66:11, 13).

"Blessed be God, even the Father of our Lord Jesus Christ, the Father of mercies, and the God of all comfort; who comforteth us in all our tribulation, that we may be able to comfort them which are in any trouble, by the comfort wherewith we ourselves are comforted of God" (2Corinthians 1:3, 4).

Hope

"Every man that hath this hope in him purifieth himself, even as he is pure" (1John 3:3).

"Be of good courage, and he shall strengthen your heart, all ye that hope in the LORD" (Psalm 31:24).

"Why art thou cast down, O my soul? and why art thou disquieted within me? hope thou in God: for I shall yet praise him, who is the health of my countenance, and my God' (Psalm 42:11).

"That by two immutable things, in which it was impossible for God to lie, we might have a strong consolation, who have fled for refuge to lay hold upon the hope set before us: which hope we have as an anchor of the soul, both sure and stedfast, and which entereth into that within the veil" (Hebrews 6:18, 19).

"Blessed be the God and Father of our Lord Jesus Christ, which according to his abundant mercy hath begotten us again unto a lively hope by the resurrection of Jesus Christ... Wherefore gird up the loins of your mind, be sober, and hope to the end... that your faith and hope might be in God" (1Peter 1:3, 13, 21).

"Thou art my trust from my youth" (Psalm 71:5).

"In the multitude of my thoughts within me thy comforts delight my soul" (Psalm 94:19).

"The hope which is laid up for you in heaven... The hope of the Gospel... The hope of glory" (Colossians 1:5, 23, 27).

23. Delight And Joy In God

"The joy of the LORD is your strength" (Nehemiah 8:10).

"Ye shall go out with joy, and be led forth with peace" (Isaiah 55:12).

"Let the righteous be glad; let them rejoice before God: yea, let them exceedingly rejoice" (Psalm 68:3).

"Thou hast put gladness in my heart, more than in the time that their corn and their wine increased" (Psalm 4:7).

"The righteous shall be glad in the LORD, and shall trust in him; and all the upright in heart shall glory" (Psalm 64:10).

"My soul shall be satisfied as with marrow and fatness; and my mouth shall praise thee with joyful lips" (Psalm 63:5).

"Behold, my servants shall sing for joy of heart" (Isaiah 65:14).

"The voice of rejoicing and salvation is in the tabernacles of the righteous" (Psalm 118:15).

"Light is sown for the righteous, and gladness for the upright in heart" (Psalm 97:11).

"Then shalt thou have thy delight in the Almighty, and shalt lift up thy face unto God" (Job 22:26).

"They that sow in tears shall reap in joy. 6 He that goeth forth and weepeth, bearing precious seed, shall doubtless come again with rejoicing, bringing his sheaves with him" (Psalm 126:5, 6).

"Blessed is the people that know the joyful sound: they shall walk, O LORD, in the light of thy countenance. In thy name shall they rejoice all the day: and in thy righteousness shall they be exalted" (Psalm 89:15, 16).

"or confusion they shall rejoice in their portion: therefore in their land they shall possess the double: everlasting joy shall be unto them. I will greatly rejoice in the LORD, my soul shall be joyful in my God" (Isaiah 61:7, 10).

"[We] rejoice in hope of the glory of God" (Romans 5:2).

"Thou shalt rejoice in the LORD, and shalt glory in the Holy One of Israel" (Isaiah 41:16).

"Our heart shall rejoice in him, because we have trusted in his holy name" (Psalm 33:21).

"We will be glad and rejoice in thee, we will remember thy love more than wine" (Song of Solomon 1:4).

"I will see you again, and your heart shall rejoice, and your joy no man taketh from you" (John 16:22).

"They joy before thee according to the joy in harvest, and as men rejoice when they divide the spoil" (Isaiah 9:3).

"Whom having not seen, ye love; in whom, though now ye see him not, yet believing, ye rejoice with joy unspeakable and full of glory" (1Peter 1:8).

"The redeemed of the LORD shall return, and come with singing unto Zion; and everlasting joy shall be upon their head: they shall obtain gladness and joy; and sorrow and mourning shall flee away" (Isaiah 51:11).

"I will rejoice in the LORD, I will joy in the God of my salvation" (Habakkuk 3:18).

"These things have I spoken unto you, that my joy might remain in you, and that your joy might be full" (John 15:11).

24. Support In Death

"The righteous hath hope in his death" (Proverbs 14:32).

"Mark the perfect man, and behold the upright: for the end of that man is peace" (Psalm 37:37).

"God will redeem my soul from the power of the grave: for he shall receive me" (Psalm 49:15).

"For this God is our God for ever and ever: he will be our guide even unto death" (Psalm 48:14).

"My flesh and my heart faileth: but God is the strength of my heart, and my portion for ever" (Psalm 73:26).

"For I am persuaded, that neither death, nor life, nor angels, nor principalities, nor powers, nor things present, nor things to come, nor height, nor depth, nor any other creature, shall be able to separate us from the love of God, which is in Christ Jesus our Lord" (Romans 8:38, 39).

"He will swallow up death in victory; and the Lord GOD will wipe away tears from off all faces" (Isaiah 25:8).

"For which cause we faint not; but though our outward man perish, yet the inward man is renewed day by day" (2Corinthians 4:16).

"I know whom I have believed, and am persuaded that he is able to keep that which I have committed unto him against that day" (2Timothy 1:12).

"Yea, though I walk through the valley of the shadow of death, I will fear no evil: for thou art with me; thy rod and thy staff they comfort me" (Psalm 23:4).

"I will ransom them from the power of the grave; I will redeem them from death: O death, I will be thy plagues; O grave, I will be thy destruction" (Hosea 13:14).

"O death, where is thy sting? O grave, where is thy victory? Thanks be to God, which giveth us the victory through our Lord Jesus Christ" (1Corinthians 15:55, 57).

"That through death he might destroy him that had the power of death, that is, the devil; and deliver them who through fear of death were all their lifetime subject to bondage" (Hebrews 2:14, 15).

Chapter 4

Promises Of Blessings In The Future World

1. Deliverance From Hell

"Israel shall be saved in the LORD with an everlasting salvation: ye shall not be ashamed nor confounded world without end" (Isaiah 45:17).

"Righteousness delivereth from death" (Proverbs 10:2; 11:4).

"The way of life is above to the wise, that he may depart from hell beneath" (Proverbs 15:24).

"Great is thy mercy toward me: and thou hast delivered my soul from the lowest hell" (Psalm 86:13).

"Much more then, being now justified by his blood, we shall be saved from wrath through him" (Romans 5:9).

"If a man keep my saying, he shall never see death" (John 8:51).

"Jesus, which delivered us from the wrath to come" (1Thessalonians 1:10).

"That whosoever believeth in him should not perish, but have everlasting life" (John 3:16).

"God hath not appointed us to wrath, but to obtain salvation by our Lord Jesus Christ" (1Thessalonians 5:9).

"Blessed and holy is he that hath part in the first resurrection: on such the second death hath no power" (Revelation 20:6).

2. Happiness Immediately After Death

"He shall enter into peace: they shall rest in their beds, each one walking in his uprightness" (Isaiah 57:2).

"We are confident, I say, and willing rather to be absent from the body, and to be present with the Lord" (2Corinthians 5:8).

"Abraham said, Son, remember that thou in thy lifetime receivedst thy good things, and likewise Lazarus evil things: but now he is comforted, and thou art tormented" (Luke 16:25).

"Thou shalt guide me with thy counsel, and afterward receive me to glory" (Psalm 73:24).

"God will redeem my soul from the power of the grave: for he shall receive me" (Psalm 49:15).

"Jesus said unto him, Verily I say unto thee, To day shalt thou be with me in paradise" (Luke 23:43).

"For to me to live is Christ, and to die is gain. Having a desire to depart, and to be with Christ; which is far better" (Philippians 1:21, 23).

"Ye are come unto mount Sion, and unto the city of the living God, the heavenly Jerusalem, and to God the Judge of all, and to the spirits of just men made perfect" (Hebrews 12:22, 23).

"There the wicked cease from troubling; and there the weary be at rest. There the prisoners rest together; they hear not the voice of the oppressor" (Job 3:17, 18).

"Blessed are the dead which die in the Lord from henceforth: Yea, saith the Spirit, that they may rest from their labours; and their works do follow them" (Revelation 14:13).

3. A Glorious Resurrection

"Many of them that sleep in the dust of the earth shall awake, some to everlasting life, and some to shame and everlasting contempt" (Daniel 12:2).

"My flesh also shall rest in hope. For thou wilt not leave my soul in hell; neither wilt thou suffer thine Holy One to see corruption" (Psalm 16:9, 10).

"Thy dead men shall live, together with my dead body shall they arise. Awake and sing, ye that dwell in dust: for thy dew is as the dew of herbs, and the earth shall cast out the dead" (Isaiah 26:19).

"The hour is coming, in the which all that are in the graves shall hear his voice, and shall come forth; they that have done good, unto the resurrection of life; and they that have done evil, unto the resurrection of damnation" (John 5:28, 29).

"They which shall be accounted worthy to obtain that world, and the resurrection from the dead, neither marry, nor are given in marriage: Neither can they die any more: for they are equal unto the angels; and are the children of God, being the children of the resurrection" (Luke 20:35, 36).

"Though after my skin worms destroy this body, yet in my flesh shall I see God: whom I shall see for myself, and mine eyes shall behold, and not another; though my reins be consumed within me" (Job 19:26, 27).

"This is the Father's will which hath sent me, that of all which he hath given me I should lose nothing, but should raise it up again at the last day. And this is the will of him that sent me, that every one which seeth the Son, and believeth on him, may have everlasting life: and I will raise him up at the last day. Whoso eateth my flesh, and drinketh my blood, hath eternal life; and I will raise him up at the last day" (John 6:39, 40, 54).

"We know that if our earthly house of this tabernacle were dissolved, we have a building of God, an house not made with hands, eternal in the heavens. For in this we groan, earnestly desiring to be clothed upon with our house which is from heaven: If so be that being clothed we shall not be found naked. For we that are in this tabernacle do groan, being burdened: not for that we would be unclothed, but clothed upon, that mortality might be swallowed up of life" (2Corinthians 5:1-4).

"If the Spirit of him that raised up Jesus from the dead dwell in you, he that raised up Christ from the dead shall also quicken your mortal bodies by his Spirit that dwelleth in you" (Romans 8:11).

"Since by man came death, by man came also the resurrection of the dead. So also is the resurrection of the dead. It is sown in corruption; it is raised in incorruption: it is sown in dishonour; it is raised in glory: it is sown in weakness; it is raised in power: it is sown a natural body; it is raised a spiritual body. As we have borne the image of the earthy, we shall also bear the image of the heavenly. Behold, I shew you a mystery; We shall not all sleep, but we shall all be changed, in a moment, in the twinkling of an eye, at the last trump: for the trumpet shall sound, and the dead shall be raised incorruptible, and we shall be changed. For this corruptible must put on incorruption, and this mortal must put on immortality. So when this corruptible shall have put on incorruption, and this mortal shall have put on immortality, then shall be brought to pass the saying that is written, Death is swallowed up in victory" (1Corinthians 15:21, 42-44, 49, 51-54).

"I am the resurrection, and the life: he that believeth in me, though he were dead, yet shall he live" (John 11:25).

"He which raised up the Lord Jesus shall raise up us also by Jesus, and shall present us with you" (2Corinthians 4:14).

"Do ye not know that the saints shall judge the world?... Know ye not that we shall judge angels?" (1Corinthians 6:2, 3).

"Who shall change our vile body, that it may be fashioned like unto his glorious body, according to the working whereby he is able even to subdue all things unto himself" (Philippians 3:21).

"If we believe that Jesus died and rose again, even so them also which sleep in Jesus will God bring with him. For this we say unto you by the word of the Lord, that we which are alive and remain unto the coming of the Lord shall not prevent them which are asleep. For the Lord himself shall descend from heaven with a shout, with the voice of the archangel, and with the trump of God: and the dead in Christ shall rise first: then we which are alive and remain shall be caught up together with them in the clouds, to meet the Lord in the air: and so shall we ever be with the Lord" (1Thessalonians 4:14-17).

"Jesus Christ, who hath abolished death, and hath brought life and immortality to light through the gospel" (2Timothy 1:10).

4. Everlasting Happiness In Heaven

"To them who by patient continuance in well doing seek for glory and honour and immortality, eternal life" (Romans 2:7).

"We shall be saved by his life. They which receive abundance of grace and of the gift of righteousness shall reign in life by one, Jesus Christ" (Romans 5:10, 17).

"That ye may be counted worthy of the kingdom of God, for which ye also suffer: To you who are troubled rest with us, when the Lord Jesus shall be revealed from heaven with his mighty angels. He shall come to be glorified in his saints, and to be admired in all them that believe (because our testimony among you was believed) in that day. That the name of our Lord Jesus Christ may be glorified in you, and ye in him, according to the grace of our God and the Lord Jesus Christ" (2Thessalonians 1:5, 7, 10, 12).

"There remaineth therefore a rest to the people of God" (Hebrews 4:9).

"The upright shall have dominion over them in the morning" (Psalm 49:14).

"We, according to his promise, look for new heavens and a new earth, wherein dwelleth righteousness" (2Peter 3:13).

"Thou hast a few names even in Sardis which have not defiled their garments; and they shall walk with me in white: for they are worthy" (Revelation 3:4).

"In my Father's house are many mansions: if it were not so, I would have told you. I go to prepare a place for you. And if I go and prepare a place for you, I will come again, and receive you unto myself; that where I am, there ye may be also" (John 14:2, 3).

"By faith he sojourned in the land of promise, as in a strange country, dwelling in tabernacles with Isaac and Jacob, the heirs with him of the same promise: For he looked for a city which hath foundations, whose builder and maker is God. They desire a better country, that is, an heavenly: wherefore God is not ashamed to be called their God: for he hath prepared for them a city" (Hebrews 11:9, 10, 16).

"There shall be no night there; and they need no candle, neither light of the sun; for the Lord God giveth them light: and they shall reign for ever and ever" (Revelation 22:5; Isaiah 60:20).

"Receiving the end of your faith, even the salvation of your souls. Gird up the loins of your mind, be sober, and hope to the end for the grace that is to be brought unto you at the revelation of Jesus Christ" (1Peter 1:9, 13).

"He is the Mediator of the new testament, that by means of death, for the redemption of the transgressions that were under the first testament, they which are called might receive the promise of eternal inheritance" (Hebrews 9:15).

"They before the throne of God, and serve him day and night in his temple: and he that sitteth on the throne shall dwell among them. They shall hunger no more, neither thirst any more; neither shall the sun light on them, nor any heat. For the Lamb which is in the midst of the throne shall feed them, and shall lead them unto living fountains of waters: and God shall wipe away all tears from their eyes" (Revelation 7:15-17).

"Eye hath not seen, nor ear heard, neither have entered into the heart of man, the things which God hath prepared for them that love him" (1Corinthians 2:9).

"Beloved, now are we the sons of God, and it doth not yet appear what we shall be: but we know that, when he shall appear, we shall be like him; for we shall see him as he is" (1John 3:2).

"Thy wrath is come, and the time of the dead, that they should be judged, and that thou shouldest give reward unto thy servants the prophets, and to the saints, and them that fear thy name, small and great" (Revelation 11:18).

"The glory which thou gavest me I have given them; that they may be one, even as we are one. Father, I will that they also, whom thou hast given me, be with me where I am; that they may behold my glory" (John 17:22, 24).

"I saw no temple therein: for the Lord God Almighty and the Lamb are the temple of it. The city had no need of the sun, neither of the moon, to shine in it: for the glory of God did lighten it, and the Lamb is the light thereof" (Revelation 21:22, 23).

"Be thou faithful unto death, and I will give thee a crown of life" (Revelation 2:10).

Freedom From All Sorrow In Heaven

"And there shall be no more curse" (Revelation 22:3).

"The LORD shall be thine everlasting light, and the days of thy mourning shall be ended" (Isaiah 60:20).

"Treasures in heaven, where neither moth nor rust doth corrupt, and where thieves do not break through nor steal" (Matthew 6:20).

"God shall wipe away all tears from their eyes; and there shall be no more death, neither sorrow, nor crying, neither shall there be any more pain: for the former things are passed away" (Revelation 21:4).

Joy In Heaven

"I will make thee ruler over many things: enter thou into the joy of thy Lord" (Matthew 25:21).

"[He] is able to keep you from falling, and to present you faultless before the presence of his glory with exceeding joy" (Jude 24).

"Thou wilt shew me the path of life: in thy presence is fulness of joy; at thy right hand there are pleasures for evermore" (Psalm 16:11).

Glory In Heaven

"Then shall the righteous shine forth as the sun in the kingdom of their Father" (Matthew 13:43).

"That, when his glory shall be revealed, ye may be glad also with exceeding joy" (1Peter 4:13).

"When Christ, who is our life, shall appear, then shall ye also appear with him in glory" (Colossians 3:4).

"For the elect's sakes, that they may also obtain the salvation which is in Christ Jesus with eternal glory" (2Timothy 2:10).

"If children, then heirs; heirs of God, and joint-heirs with Christ; if so be that we suffer with him, that we may be also glorified together. The sufferings of this present time are not worthy to be compared with the glory which shall be revealed in us" (Romans 8:17, 18).

"Our light affliction, which is but for a moment, worketh for us a far more exceeding and eternal weight of glory; while we look not at the things which are seen, but at the things which are not seen: for the things which are seen are temporal; but the things which are not seen are eternal" (2Corinthians 4:17, 18).

"They that be wise shall shine as the brightness of the firmament; and they that turn many to righteousness as the stars for ever and ever" (Daniel 12:3).

The Kingdom Of Heaven

"It is your Father's good pleasure to give you the kingdom" (Luke 12:32).

"The Lord shall deliver me from every evil work, and will preserve me unto his heavenly kingdom" (2Timothy 4:18).

"Come, ye blessed of my Father, inherit the kingdom prepared for you from the foundation of the world" (Matthew 25:34).

"An entrance shall be ministered unto you abundantly into the everlasting kingdom of our Lord and Saviour Jesus Christ" (2Peter 1:11).

"I appoint unto you a kingdom, as my Father hath appointed unto me; that ye may eat and drink at my table in my kingdom, and sit on thrones judging the twelve tribes of Israel" (Luke 22:29, 30).

The Heavenly Inheritance

"The eyes of your understanding being enlightened; that ye may know what is the hope of his calling, and what the riches of the glory of his inheritance in the saints" (Ephesians 1:18).

"[Who] hath begotten us again unto a lively hope by the resurrection of Jesus Christ from the dead, to an inheritance incorruptible, and undefiled, and that fadeth not away, reserved in heaven for you" (1Peter 1:3, 4).

Enjoyment Of God

"So shall we ever be with the Lord" (1Thessalonians 4:17).

"With thee is the fountain of life: in thy light shall we see light" (Psalm 36:9).

"As for me, I will behold thy face in righteousness: I shall be satisfied, when I awake, with thy likeness" (Psalm 17:15).

"The throne of God and of the Lamb shall be in it; and his servants shall serve him. And they shall see his face; and his name shall be in their foreheads" (Revelation 22:3, 4).

Eternal Life

"But the righteous into life eternal" (Matthew 25:46).

"This is the promise that he hath promised us, even eternal life" (1John 2:25).

"Verily, verily, I say unto you, He that believeth on me hath everlasting life" (John 6:47). See verses 51, 54.

"The gift of God is eternal life through Jesus Christ our Lord" (Romans 6:23).

"He that soweth to the Spirit shall of the Spirit reap life everlasting" (Galatians 6:8).

"Neither can they die any more: for they are equal unto the angels" (Luke 20:36).

"In hope of eternal life, which God, that cannot lie, promised before the world began" (Titus 1:2).

"My sheep hear my voice, and I know them, and they follow me: and I give unto them eternal life" (John 10:27, 28).

"Jesus said unto her, I am the resurrection, and the life: whosoever liveth and believeth in me shall never die" (John 11:25, 26).

"To them who by patient continuance in well doing seek for glory and honour and immortality, eternal life" (Romans 2:7).

"God hath given to us eternal life, and this life is in his Son. That ye may know that ye have eternal life" (1John 5:11, 13).

"For God so loved the world, that he gave his only begotten Son, that whosoever believeth in him should not perish, but have everlasting life" (John 3:16).

PART TWO

Promises For The Exercise Of Duties And Glories

Chapter 1

In The Fulfillment Of Duty Toward God

1. To Faith In Christ

"Behold, I lay in Zion for a foundation a stone, a tried stone, a precious corner stone, a sure foundation: he that believeth shall not make haste" (Isaiah 28:16).

"He that believeth on him shall not be confounded" (1Peter 2:6).

"I am come a light into the world, that whosoever believeth on me should not abide in darkness" (John 12:46).

"God so loved the world, that he gave his only begotten Son, that whosoever believeth in him should not perish, but have everlasting life. He that believeth on him is not condemned. He that believeth on the Son hath everlasting life" (John 3:16, 18, 36; 6:47).

"By grace are ye saved through faith" (Ephesians 2:8).

"Thy faith hath saved thee; go in peace" (Luke 7:50).

"Look unto me, and be ye saved, all the ends of the earth" (Isaiah 45:22).

"If thou canst believe, all things are possible to him that believeth" (Mark 9:23).

"Christ is the end of the law for righteousness to every one that believeth" (Romans 10:4).

"Believe on the Lord Jesus Christ, and thou shalt be saved, and thy house" (Acts 16:31).

"Behold, I lay in Sion a stumblingstone and rock of offence: and whosoever believeth on him shall not be ashamed" (Romans 9:33).

"To him that worketh not, but believeth on him that justifieth the ungodly, his faith is counted for righteousness" (Romans 4:5).

"To him give all the prophets witness, that through his name whosoever believeth in him shall receive remission of sins" (Acts 10:43).

"Come unto me, all ye that labour and are heavy laden, and I will give you rest" (Matthew 11:28).

"The just shall live by faith. We are not of them who draw back unto perdition; but of them that believe to the saving of the soul" (Hebrews 10:38, 39).

"And Jesus said unto them, I am the bread of life: he that cometh to me shall never hunger; and he that believeth on me shall never thirst. All that the Father giveth me shall come to me; and him that cometh to me I will in no wise cast out" (John 6:35, 37).

"They which be of faith are blessed with faithful Abraham. They which are of faith, the same are the children of Abraham. The Scripture hath concluded all under sin, that the promise by faith of Jesus Christ might be given to them that believe" (Galatians 3:9, 7, 22).

"To whom coming, as unto a living stone, disallowed indeed of men, but chosen of God, and precious, ye also, as lively stones, are built up a spiritual house, an holy priesthood, to offer up spiritual sacrifices, acceptable to God by Jesus Christ" (1Peter 2:4, 5). See Justification, part 1, chap. 3, sect. 2.

"Blessed are they that have not seen, and yet have believed" (John 20:29).

"We trust in the living God, who is the Saviour of all men, specially of those that believe" (1Timothy 4:10).

"That ye be not slothful, but followers of them who through faith and patience inherit the promises" (Hebrews 6:12).

"As many as received him, to them gave he power to become the sons of God, even to them that believe on his name" (John 1:12).

Confessing Christ

"Whosoever shall confess that Jesus is the Son of God, God dwelleth in him, and he in God" (1John 4:15).

"Whosoever therefore shall confess me before men, him will I confess also before my Father which is in heaven" (Matthew 10:32).

"If thou shalt confess with thy mouth the Lord Jesus, and shalt believe in thine heart that God hath raised him from the dead, thou shalt be saved. For with the heart man believeth unto righteousness; and with the mouth confession is made unto salvation" (Romans 10:9, 10).

2. To Repentance

"That they may return every man from his evil way; that I may forgive their iniquity and their sin" (Jeremiah 36:3).

"Turn ye unto me, saith the LORD of hosts, and I will turn unto you, saith the LORD of hosts" (Zechariah 1:3; Malachi 3:7).

"The LORD your God is gracious and merciful, and will not turn away his face from you, if ye return unto him" (2Chronicles 30:9).

"O Jerusalem, wash thine heart from wickedness, that thou mayest be saved. How long shall thy vain thoughts lodge within thee?" (Jeremiah 4:14).

"If my people, which are called by my name, shall humble themselves, and pray, and seek my face, and turn from their wicked ways; then will I hear from heaven, and will forgive their sin" (2Chronicles 7:14).

"If so be they will hearken, and turn every man from his evil way, that I may repent me of the evil, which I purpose to do unto them because of the evil of their doings. Amend your ways and your doings, and obey the voice of the LORD your God; and the LORD will repent him of the evil that he hath pronounced against you" (Jeremiah 26:3, 13).

"If that nation, against whom I have pronounced, turn from their evil, I will repent of the evil that I thought to do unto them" (Jeremiah 18:8).

"Let the wicked forsake his way, and the unrighteous man his thoughts: and let him return unto the LORD, and he will have mercy upon him; and to our God, for he will abundantly pardon" (Isaiah 55:7).

"If the wicked will turn from all his sins that he hath committed, and keep all my statutes, and do that which is lawful and right, he shall surely live, he shall not die. All his transgressions that he hath committed, they shall not be mentioned unto him: in his righteousness that he hath done he shall live. Have I any pleasure at all that the wicked should die? saith the Lord GOD: and not that he should return from his ways, and live? Repent, and turn yourselves from all your transgressions; so iniquity shall not be your ruin. Cast away from you all your transgressions, whereby ye have transgressed; and make you a new heart and a new spirit: for why will ye die, O house of Israel? For I have no pleasure in the death of him that dieth, saith the Lord GOD: wherefore turn yourselves, and live ye" (Ezekiel 18:21-23; 30-32).

"Depart from evil, and do good; and dwell for evermore" (Psalm 37:27).

"Turn you at my reproof: behold, I will pour out my spirit unto you, I will make known my words unto you" (Proverbs 1:23).

"Turn ye even to me with all your heart, and with fasting, and with weeping, and with mourning: and rend your heart, and not your garments, and turn unto the LORD your God: for he is gracious and merciful, slow to anger, and of great kindness, and repenteth him of the evil. Who knoweth if he will return and repent, and leave a blessing behind him; even a meat offering and a drink offering unto the LORD your God?" (Joel 2:12-14).

"When I say unto the wicked, Thou shalt surely die; if he turn from his sin, and do that which is lawful and right; if the wicked restore the pledge, give again that he had robbed, walk in the statutes of life, without committing iniquity; he shall surely live, he shall not die. None of his sins that he hath committed shall be mentioned unto him: he hath done that which is lawful and right. If the wicked turn from his wickedness, and do that which is lawful and right, he shall live thereby" (Ezekiel 33:14-16, 19).

"If thou return to the Almighty, thou shalt be built up, thou shalt put away iniquity far from thy tabernacles" (Job 22:23).

"Awake thou that sleepest, and arise from the dead, and Christ shall give thee light" (Ephesians 5:14).

"Repent, and be baptized every one of you in the name of Jesus Christ for the remission of sins, and ye shall receive the gift of the Holy Ghost" (Acts 2:38).

"Repent ye therefore, and be converted, that your sins may be blotted out, when the times of refreshing shall come from the presence of the Lord" (Acts 3:19).

To Them That Mourn For The Wickedness Of The Land

"Go through the midst of the city, through the midst of Jerusalem, and set a mark upon the foreheads of the men that sigh and that cry for all the abominations that be done in the midst thereof. Slay utterly old and young, both maids, and little children, and women: but come not near any man upon whom is the mark" (Ezekiel 9:4, 6).

Repenting In Affliction

"Come, and let us return unto the LORD: for he hath torn, and he will heal us; he hath smitten, and he will bind us up" (Hosea 6:1).

"He looketh upon men, and if any say, I have sinned, and perverted that which was right, and it profited me not; 28 He will deliver his soul from going into the pit, and his life shall see the light" (Job 33:27, 28).

"When thou art in tribulation, and all these things are come upon thee, even in the latter days, if thou turn to the LORD thy God, and shalt be obedient unto his voice; (for the LORD thy God is a merciful God;) he will not forsake thee, neither destroy thee, nor forget the covenant of thy fathers which he sware unto them" (Deuteronomy 4:30, 31).

Confession Of Sin

"Whoso confesseth and forsaketh them shall have mercy" (Proverbs 28:13).

"I said, I will confess my transgressions unto the LORD; and thou forgavest the iniquity of my sin. Thou art my hiding place; thou shalt preserve me" (Psalm 32:5, 7).

"If we confess our sins, he is faithful and just to forgive us our sins, and to cleanse us from all unrighteousness" (1John 1:9).

"The son said unto him, Father, I have sinned against heaven, and in thy sight, and am no more worthy to be called thy son. But the father said to his servants, Bring forth the best robe, and put it on him; and put a ring on his hand, and shoes on his feet" (Luke 15:21, 22).

"If they shall confess their iniquity, and the iniquity of their fathers, with their trespass which they trespassed against me, and that also they have walked contrary unto me; and that I also have walked contrary unto them, and have brought them into the land of their enemies; if then their uncircumcised hearts be humbled, and they then accept of the punishment of their iniquity: then will I remember my covenant with Jacob, and also my covenant with Isaac, and also my covenant with Abraham will I remember; and I will remember the land" (Leviticus 26:40-42).

"Return, thou backsliding Israel, saith the LORD; and I will not cause mine anger to fall upon you: for I am merciful, saith the LORD, and I will not keep anger for ever. Only acknowledge thine iniquity, that thou hast transgressed against the LORD thy God, and hast scattered thy ways to the strangers under every green tree, and ye have not obeyed my voice, saith the LORD" (Jeremiah 3:12, 13).

3. Obedience

"Blessed are they that keep judgment, and he that doeth righteousness at all times" (Psalm 106:3).

"Whosoever shall do and teach them, the same shall be called great in the kingdom of heaven" (Matthew 5:19).

"Hearken, O Israel, unto the statutes and unto the judgments, which I teach you, for to do them, that ye may live, and go in and possess the land which the LORD God of your fathers giveth you. Keep therefore and do them; for this is your wisdom and your understanding in the sight of the nations, which shall hear all these statutes, and say, Surely this great nation is a wise and understanding people" (Deuteronomy 4:1, 6).

"Keep therefore the words of this covenant, and do them, that ye may prosper in all that ye do" (Deuteronomy 29:9).

"A blessing, if ye obey the commandments of the LORD your God, which I command you this day" (Deuteronomy 11:27).

"O that there were such an heart in them, that they would fear me, and keep all my commandments always, that it might be well with them, and with their children for ever!" (Deuteronomy 5:29).

"It shall come to pass, if ye hearken to these judgments, and keep, and do them, that the LORD thy God shall keep unto thee the covenant and the mercy which he sware unto thy fathers" (Deuteronomy 7:12).

"Hear therefore, O Israel, and observe to do it; that it may be well with thee, and that ye may increase mightily, as the LORD God of thy fathers hath promised thee, in the land that floweth with milk and honey. Thou shalt do that which is right and good in the sight of the LORD: that it may be well with thee, and that thou mayest go in and possess the good land which the LORD sware unto thy fathers, to cast out all thine enemies from before thee, as the LORD hath spoken" (Deuteronomy 6:3, 18, 19).

"Ye shall do my statutes, and keep my judgments, and do them; and ye shall dwell in the land in safety. And the land shall yield her fruit, and ye shall eat your fill, and dwell therein in safety" (Leviticus 25:18, 19).

"If ye will fear the LORD, and serve him, and obey his voice, and not rebel against the commandment of the LORD, then shall both ye and also the king that reigneth over you continue following the LORD your God" (1Samuel 12:14).

"Set your hearts unto all the words which I testify among you this day, which ye shall command your children to observe to do, all the words of this law. For it is not a vain thing for you; because it is your life: and through this thing ye shall prolong your days in the land, whither ye go over Jordan to possess it" (Deuteronomy 32:46, 47).

"That the LORD may turn from the fierceness of his anger, and shew thee mercy, and have compassion upon thee, and multiply thee, as he hath sworn unto thy fathers; when thou shalt hearken to the voice of the LORD thy God, to keep all his commandments which I command thee this day, to do that which is right in the eyes of the LORD thy God" (Deuteronomy 13:17, 18).

"Be ye strong therefore, and let not your hands be weak: for your work shall be rewarded" (2Chronicles 15:7).

"All the paths of the LORD are mercy and truth unto such as keep his covenant and his testimonies" (Psalm 25:10).

"If they obey and serve him, they shall spend their days in prosperity, and their years in pleasures" (Job 36:11).

"If ye will obey my voice indeed, and keep my covenant, then ye shall be a peculiar treasure unto me above all people" (Exodus 19:5).

"Blessed are the undefiled in the way, who walk in the law of the LORD. Blessed are they that keep his testimonies, and that seek him with the whole heart. Then shall I not be ashamed, when I have respect unto all thy commandments" (Psalm 119:1, 2, 6).

"The LORD give thee wisdom and understanding, and give thee charge concerning Israel, that thou mayest keep the law of the LORD thy God; then shalt thou prosper, if thou takest heed to fulfil the statutes and judgments which the LORD charged Moses with concerning Israel" (1Chronicles 22:12, 13).

"He that keepeth the commandment keepeth his own soul" (Proverbs 19:16).

"O that thou hadst hearkened to my commandments! then had thy peace been as a river, and thy righteousness as the waves of the sea" (Isaiah 48:18).

"Blessed are they that do his commandments, that they may have right to the tree of life, and may enter in through the gates into the city" (Revelation 22:14).

"Obey my voice, and I will be your God, and ye shall be my people: and walk ye in all the ways that I have commanded you, that it may be well unto you" (Jeremiah 7:23).

"Keep the charge of the LORD thy God, to walk in his ways, to keep his statutes, and his commandments, and his judgments, and his testimonies, as it is written in the law of Moses, that thou mayest prosper in all that thou doest, and whithersoever thou turnest thyself" (1Kings 2:3).

"See, I have set before thee this day life and good, and death and evil; in that I command thee this day to love the LORD thy God, to walk in his ways, and to keep his commandments and his statutes and his judgments, that thou mayest live and multiply: and the LORD thy God shall bless thee" (Deuteronomy 30:15, 16).

"He that doeth the will of God abideth for ever" (1John 2:17).

"If ye know these things, happy are ye if ye do them" (John 13:17).

"To him that ordereth his conversation aright will I shew the salvation of God" (Psalm 50:23).

"If any man will do his will, he shall know of the doctrine, whether it be of God, or whether I speak of myself" (John 7:17).

"Whosoever shall do the will of my Father which is in heaven, the same is my brother, and sister, and mother" (Matthew 12:50).

"Whatsoever we ask, we receive of him, because we keep his commandments, and do those things that are pleasing in his sight" (1John 3:22).

"Not every one that saith unto me, Lord, Lord, shall enter into the kingdom of heaven; but he that doeth the will of my Father which is in heaven" (Matthew 7:21).

"Whoso looketh into the perfect law of liberty, and continueth therein, he being not a forgetful hearer, but a doer of the work, this man shall be blessed in his deed" (James 1:25).

"He that keepeth the law, happy is he" (Proverbs 29:18).

"The doers of the law shall be justified" (Romans 2:13).

"If ye be willing and obedient, ye shall eat the good of the land" (Isaiah 1:19).

"Those things, which ye have both learned, and received, and heard, and seen in me, do: and the God of peace shall be with you" (Philippians 4:9).

Obeying Christ

"If ye keep my commandments, ye shall abide in my love" (John 15:10).

"He became the author of eternal salvation unto all them that obey him" (Hebrews 5:9).

"If thou shalt indeed obey his voice, and do all that I speak; then

I will be an enemy unto thine enemies, and an adversary unto thine adversaries" (Exodus 23:22).

"Who is among you that feareth the LORD, that obeyeth the voice of his servant, that walketh in darkness, and hath no light? Let him trust in the name of the LORD, and stay upon his God" (Isaiah 50:10).

"If a man keep my saying, he shall never see death" (John 8:51).

"He that heareth my word, and believeth on him that sent me, hath everlasting life, and shall not come into condemnation; but is passed from death unto life" (John 5:24).

"Whosoever heareth these sayings of mine, and doeth them, I will liken him unto a wise man, which built his house upon a rock: and the rain descended, and the floods came, and the winds blew, and beat upon that house; and it fell not: for it was founded upon a rock" (Matthew 7:24, 25).

4. To Sincerity And Uprightness

"With an upright man thou wilt shew thyself upright" (Psalm 18:25).

"I know also, my God, that thou triest the heart, and hast pleasure in uprightness" (1Chronicles 29:17).

"The righteous LORD loveth righteousness; his countenance doth behold the upright" (Psalm 11:7).

"The eyes of the LORD run to and fro throughout the whole

earth, to shew himself strong in the behalf of them whose heart is perfect toward him" (2Chronicles 16:9).

"The way of the LORD is strength to the upright" (Proverbs 10:29).

"Righteousness keepeth him that is upright in the way" (Proverbs 13:6).

"Let my heart be sound in thy statutes; that I be not ashamed" (Psalm 119:80).

"Do good, O LORD, unto those that be good, and to them that are upright in their hearts" (Psalm 125:4).

"The LORD knoweth the days of the upright: and their inheritance shall be for ever" (Psalm 37:18).

"LORD, who shall abide in thy tabernacle? Who shall dwell in thy holy hill? He that walketh uprightly, and worketh righteousness, and speaketh the truth in his heart" (Psalm 15:1, 2).

"The integrity of the upright shall guide them. The righteousness of the upright shall deliver them. Such as are upright in their way are his delight" (Proverbs 11:3, 6, 20).

"He layeth up sound wisdom for the righteous: he is a buckler to them that walk uprightly. The upright shall dwell in the land, and the perfect shall remain in it" (Proverbs 2:7, 21).

"The prayer of the upright is his delight" (Proverbs 15:8).

"They that deal truly are his delight" (Proverbs 12:22).

"Do not my words do good to him that walketh uprightly?" (Micah 2:7).

"If our heart condemn us not, then have we confidence toward God" (1John 3:21).

"Happy is he that condemneth not himself in that thing which he alloweth" (Romans 14:22).

"The wicked shall be a ransom for the righteous, and the transgressor for the upright" (Proverbs 21:18).

"If thou wert pure and upright; surely now he would awake for thee, and make the habitation of thy righteousness prosperous" (Job 8:6).

"Whoso causeth the righteous to go astray in an evil way, he shall fall himself into his own pit: but the upright shall have good things in possession. Whoso walketh uprightly shall be saved. A faithful man shall abound with blessings" (Proverbs 28:10, 18, 20).

5. To The Love Of God

"God, that keepeth covenant and mercy for them that love him" (Nehemiah 1:5).

"All things work together for good to them that love God" (Romans 8:28).

"Because he hath set his love upon me, therefore will I deliver him" (Psalm 91:14).

"Delight thyself also in the LORD; and he shall give thee the desires of thine heart" (Psalm 37:4).

"Shewing mercy unto thousands of them that love me, and keep my commandments" (Exodus 20:6).

"God, which keepeth covenant and mercy with them that love him and keep his commandments to a thousand generations" (Deuteronomy 7:9).

"It shall come to pass, if ye shall hearken diligently unto my commandments which I command you this day, to love the LORD your God, and to serve him with all your heart and with all your soul, that I will give you the rain of your land in his due season, the first rain and the latter rain, that thou mayest gather in thy corn, and thy wine, and thine oil" (Deuteronomy 11:13, 14).

"The LORD preserveth all them that love him" (Psalm 145:20).

"If any man love God, the same is known of him" (1Corinthians 8:3).

"Let them that love him be as the sun when he goeth forth in his might" (Judges 5:31).

"Heirs of the kingdom which he hath promised to them that love him" (James 2:5).

"Eye hath not seen, nor ear heard, neither have entered into the heart of man, the things which God hath prepared for them that love him" (1Corinthians 2:9).

"O Lord, the great and dreadful God, keeping the covenant and mercy to them that love him, and to them that keep his commandments" (Daniel 9:4).

To The Love Of Christ

"He that loveth me shall be loved of my Father, and I will love him, and will manifest myself to him" (John 14:21).

"A crown of righteousness, which the Lord, the righteous judge, shall give me at that day: and not to me only, but unto all them also that love his appearing" (2Timothy 4:8).

"Grace be with all them that love our Lord Jesus Christ in sincerity" (Ephesians 6:24).

"The crown of life, which the Lord hath promised to them that love him" (James 1:12).

"I love them that love me. That I may cause those that love me to inherit substance; and I will fill their treasures" (Proverbs 8:17, 21).

6. To Trusting And Patiently Waiting On God

"He is a buckler to all those that trust in him" (Psalm 18:30).

"Blessed are all they that put their trust in him" (Psalm 2:12).

"They that trust in the LORD shall be as mount Zion, which cannot be removed, but abideth for ever" (Psalm 125:1).

"Wait on the LORD: be of good courage, and he shall strengthen thine heart: wait, I say, on the LORD" (Psalm 27:14).

"Oh how great is thy goodness, which thou hast laid up for them that fear thee; which thou hast wrought for them that trust in thee before the sons of men! Be of good courage, and he shall strengthen your heart, all ye that hope in the LORD" (Psalm 31:19, 24).

"I have trusted also in the LORD; therefore I shall not slide" (Psalm 26:1).

"The LORD is good: blessed is the man that trusteth in him" (Psalm 34:8; 84:12).

"Blessed is that man that maketh the LORD his trust, and respecteth not the proud, nor such as turn aside to lies" (Psalm 40:4).

"In God I will praise his word, in God I have put my trust; I will not fear what flesh can do unto me" (Psalm 56:4).

"Lo, this is our God; we have waited for him, and he will save us: this is the LORD; we have waited for him, we will be glad and rejoice in his salvation" (Isaiah 25:9).

"He shall not be afraid of evil tidings: his heart is fixed, trusting in the LORD. His heart is established, he shall not be afraid, until he see his desire upon his enemies" (Psalm 112:7, 8).

"Trust in the LORD, and do good; so shalt thou dwell in the land, and verily thou shalt be fed. Those that wait upon the LORD, they shall inherit the earth. The LORD shall help them, and deliver them: he shall deliver them from the wicked, and save them, because they trust in him" (Psalms 37:3, 9, 40).

"Blessed are all they that wait for him" (Isaiah 30:18).

"They shall not be ashamed that wait for me" (Isaiah 49:23).

"He that putteth his trust in the LORD shall be made fat" (Proverbs 28:25).

"Happy is he that hath the God of Jacob for his help, whose hope is in the LORD his God" (Psalm 146:5).

"Commit thy works unto the LORD, and thy thoughts shall be established. Whoso trusteth in the LORD, happy is he" (Proverbs 16:3, 20).

"Thou wilt keep him in perfect peace, whose mind is stayed on thee: because he trusteth in thee. Trust ye in the LORD for ever: for in the LORD JEHOVAH is everlasting strength" (Isaiah 26:3, 4).

"Blessed is the man that trusteth in the LORD, and whose hope the LORD is. For he shall be as a tree planted by the waters, and that spreadeth out her roots by the river, and shall not see when heat cometh, but her leaf shall be green; and shall not be careful in the year of drought, neither shall cease from yielding fruit" (Jeremiah 17:7, 8).

"We are saved by hope" (Romans 8:24).

"He knoweth them that trust in him" (Nahum 1:7).

"Whoso putteth his trust in the LORD shall be safe" (Proverbs 29:25).

"Casting all your care upon him; for he careth for you" (1Peter 5:7).

"I will look unto the LORD; I will wait for the God of my salvation: my God will hear me" (Micah 7:7).

"He that putteth his trust in me shall possess the land, and shall inherit my holy mountain" (Isaiah 57:13).

"The LORD redeemeth the soul of his servants: and none of them that trust in him shall be desolate" (Psalm 34:22).

"The LORD is good unto them that wait for him, to the soul that seeketh him. It is good that a man should both hope and quietly wait for the salvation of the LORD" (Lamentations 3:25, 26).

7. To The Fear Of God

"Surely his salvation is nigh them that fear him" (Psalm 85:9).

"He will bless them that fear the LORD, both small and great" (Psalm 115:13).

"By the fear of the LORD men depart from evil" (Proverbs 16:6).

"It shall be well with them that fear God, which fear before him" (Ecclesiastes 8:12).

"Blessed is every one that feareth the LORD; that walketh in his ways" (Psalm 128:1).

"Oh how great is thy goodness, which thou hast laid up for them that fear thee" (Psalm 31:19).

"The secret of the LORD is with them that fear him; and he will shew them his covenant" (Psalm 25:14).

"As the heaven is high above the earth, so great is his mercy toward them that fear him" (Psalm 103:11).

"Be not wise in thine own eyes: fear the LORD, and depart from evil. It shall be health to thy navel, and marrow to thy bones" (Proverbs 3:7, 8).

"In the fear of the LORD is strong confidence: and his children shall have a place of refuge. The fear of the LORD is a fountain of life, to depart from the snares of death" (Proverbs 14:26, 27).

"The LORD taketh pleasure in them that fear him" (Psalm 147:11).

"His mercy is on them that fear him from generation to generation" (Luke 1:50).

"Whosoever among you feareth God, to you is the word of this salvation sent" (Acts 13:26).

"In every nation he that feareth him, and worketh righteousness, is accepted with him" (Acts 10:35).

"Unto you that fear my name shall the Sun of righteousness arise with healing in his wings" (Malachi 4:2).

"The fear of the LORD tendeth to life: and he that hath it shall abide satisfied; he shall not be visited with evil" (Proverbs 19:23).

Honoring God

"Them that honour me I will honour" (1Samuel 2:30).

"Honour the LORD with thy substance, and with the firstfruits of all thine increase: So shall thy barns be filled with plenty, and thy presses shall burst out with new wine" (Proverbs 3:9, 10).

8. To Prayer

"The LORD is nigh unto all them that call upon him, to all that call upon him in truth" (Psalm 145:18).

"I will call upon the LORD, who is worthy to be praised: so shall I be saved from mine enemies" (Psalm 18:3).

"He shall pray unto God, and he will be favourable unto him: and he shall see his face with joy" (Job 33:26).

"LORD, thou hast heard the desire of the humble: thou wilt prepare their heart, thou wilt cause thine ear to hear" (Psalm 10:17).

"Neither shall any man desire thy land, when thou shalt go up to appear before the LORD thy God thrice in the year" (Exodus 34:24).

"What nation is there so great, who hath God so nigh unto them, as the LORD our God is in all things that we call upon him for?" (Deuteronomy 4:7).

"Thou, Lord, art good, and ready to forgive; and plenteous in mercy unto all them that call upon thee. In the day of my trouble I will call upon thee: for thou wilt answer me" (Psalms 86:5, 7).

"It is good for me to draw near to God" (Psalm 73:28).

"Draw nigh to God, and he will draw nigh to you" (James 4:8).

"Whosoever shall call on the name of the LORD shall be delivered" (Joel 2:32).

"The LORD hath heard my supplication; the LORD will receive my prayer" (Psalm 6:9).

"Call unto me, and I will answer thee, and shew thee great and mighty things, which thou knowest not" (Jeremiah 33:3).

"I will yet for this be enquired of by the house of Israel, to do it for them; I will increase them with men like a flock" (Ezekiel 36:37).

"Seeing then that we have a great high priest, that is passed into the heavens, Jesus the Son of God, let us hold fast our profession. For we have not an high priest which cannot be touched with the feeling of our infirmities; but was in all points tempted like as we are, yet without sin. Let us therefore come boldly unto the throne of grace, that we may obtain mercy, and find grace to help in time of need" (Hebrews 4:14-16). See Promises of Hearing Prayer, part 1, chap. 3, sect. 6.

"Evening, and morning, and at noon, will I pray, and cry aloud: and he shall hear my voice" (Psalm 55:17).

"Acquaint now thyself with him, and be at peace: thereby good shall come unto thee" (Job 22:21).

"The same Lord over all is rich unto all that call upon him. For whosoever shall call upon the name of the Lord shall be saved" (Romans 10:12, 13).

Seeking God

"If thou seek him, he will be found of thee" (1Chronicles 28:9).

"Ye shall seek me, and find me, when ye shall search for me with all your heart" (Jeremiah 29:13).

"If from thence thou shalt seek the LORD thy God, thou shalt find him, if thou seek him with all thy heart and with all thy soul" (Deuteronomy 4:29).

"If thou wouldest seek unto God betimes, and make thy supplication to the Almighty; if thou wert pure and upright; surely now he would awake for thee, and make the habitation of thy righteousness prosperous" (Job 8:5, 6).

"Seek ye me, and ye shall live" (Amos 5:4).

"Your heart shall live that seek God" (Psalm 69:32).

"Thou, LORD, hast not forsaken them that seek thee" (Psalm 9:10).

"I said not unto the seed of Jacob, Seek ye me in vain" (Isaiah 45:19).

"The hand of our God is upon all them for good that seek him" (Ezra 8:22).

"Seek the LORD, till he come and rain righteousness upon you" (Hosea 10:12).

"The LORD is good unto them that wait for him, to the soul that seeketh him" (Lamentations 3:25).

"That they should seek the Lord, if haply they might feel after him, and find him" (Acts 17:27).

"The LORD is with you, while ye be with him; and if ye seek him, he will be found of you" (2Chronicles 15:2).

"He that cometh to God must believe that he is, and that he is a rewarder of them that diligently seek him" (Hebrews 11:6).

Secret Prayer

"Thou, when thou prayest, enter into thy closet, and when thou hast shut thy door, pray to thy Father which is in secret; and thy

Father which seeth in secret shall reward thee openly" (Matthew 6:6).

Praising God

"Praise the LORD; for the LORD is good: sing praises unto his name; for it is pleasant" (Psalm 135:3).

"I will praise the name of God with a song, and will magnify him with thanksgiving. This also shall please the LORD better than an ox or bullock that hath horns and hoofs" (Psalm 69:30, 31).

"It is a good thing to give thanks unto the LORD, and to sing praises unto thy name, O most High: to shew forth thy lovingkindness in the morning, and thy faithfulness every night" (Psalm 92:1, 2).

Desires Of Grace

"Open thy mouth wide, and I will fill it" (Psalm 81:10).

"I am Alpha and Omega, the beginning and the end. I will give unto him that is athirst of the fountain of the water of life freely" (Revelation 21:6).

"Blessed are they which do hunger and thirst after righteousness: for they shall be filled" (Matthew 5:6).

"And let him that is athirst come. And whosoever will, let him take the water of life freely" (Revelation 22:17).

"Ho, every one that thirsteth, come ye to the waters, and he that hath no money; come ye, buy, and eat; yea, come, buy wine and milk without money and without price" (Isaiah 55:1).

"Jesus stood and cried, saying, If any man thirst, let him come unto me, and drink. He that believeth on me, as the Scripture hath said, out of his belly shall flow rivers of living water" (John 7:37, 38).

9. To wisdom and knowledge

To the wise

"Whoso findeth me [wisdom] findeth life, and shall obtain favour of the LORD" (Proverbs 8:35).

"A wise man will hear, and will increase learning; and a man of understanding shall attain unto wise counsels: to understand a proverb, and the interpretation; the words of the wise, and their dark sayings" (Proverbs 1:5, 6).

"Good understanding giveth favour" (Proverbs 13:15).

"If thou be wise, thou shalt be wise for thyself" (Proverbs 9:12).

"He is in the way of life that keepeth instruction: but he that refuseth reproof erreth" (Proverbs 10:17).

"Forsake her not, and she shall preserve thee: love her, and she shall keep thee. Exalt her, and she shall promote thee: she shall bring thee to honour, when thou dost embrace her. She shall give to thine head an ornament of grace: a crown of glory shall she deliver to thee" (Proverbs 4:6, 8, 9).

"Happy is the man that findeth wisdom, and the man that getteth understanding. For the merchandise of it is better than the merchandise of silver, and the gain thereof than fine gold. She is more precious than rubies: and all the things thou canst desire are not to be compared unto her. Length of days is in her right hand; and in her left hand riches and honour. Her ways are ways of pleasantness, and all her paths are peace. She is a tree of life to them that lay hold upon her: and happy is every one that retaineth her. The wise shall inherit glory" (Proverbs 3:13-18, 35).

"The fool shall be servant to the wise of heart" (Proverbs 11:29).

"There is treasure to be desired and oil in the dwelling of the wise" (Proverbs 21:20).

"He that getteth wisdom loveth his own soul: he that keepeth understanding shall find good" (Proverbs 19:8).

"He that handleth a matter wisely shall find good. Understanding is a wellspring of life unto him that hath it" (Proverbs 16:20, 22).

"Wisdom is a defence, and money is a defence: but the excellency of knowledge is, that wisdom giveth life to them that have it" (Ecclesiastes 7:12).

"Through wisdom is an house builded; and by understanding it is established: and by knowledge shall the chambers be filled with all precious and pleasant riches. A wise man is strong; yea, a man of knowledge increaseth strength. My son, eat thou honey, because it is good; and the honeycomb, which is sweet to thy taste: so shall the knowledge of wisdom be unto thy soul: when thou hast found it, then there shall be a reward, and thy expectation shall not be cut off" (Proverbs 24:3-5, 13, 14).

"Wisdom is profitable to direct" (Ecclesiastes 10:10).

"Whoso walketh wisely, he shall be delivered" (Proverbs 28:26).

"A man shall be commended according to his wisdom" (Proverbs 12:8).

"The way of life is above to the wise, that he may depart from hell beneath" (Proverbs 15:24).

"A man's wisdom maketh his face to shine, and the boldness of his face shall be changed" (Ecclesiastes 8:1).

"He giveth wisdom unto the wise, and knowledge to them that know understanding" (Daniel 2:21).

"Who is wise, and he shall understand these things? prudent, and he shall know them?" (Hosea 14:9).

"They that be wise shall shine as the brightness of the firmament. The wise shall understand" (Daniel 12:3, 10).

"Whoso is wise, and will observe these things, even they shall understand the lovingkindness of the LORD" (Psalm 107:43).

Love And Study Of Wisdom

"Then shall we know, if we follow on to know the LORD" (Hosea 6:3).

"I love them that love me; and those that seek me early shall find me" (Proverbs 8:17).

"Take fast hold of instruction; let her not go: keep her; for she is thy life" (Proverbs 4:13).

"Hear counsel, and receive instruction, that thou mayest be wise in thy latter end" (Proverbs 19:20).

"If thou criest after knowledge, and liftest up thy voice for understanding; if thou seekest her as silver, and searchest for her as for hid treasures; then shalt thou understand the fear of the LORD, and find the knowledge of God" (Proverbs 2:3-5).

"And God said to Solomon, Because this was in thine heart, and thou hast not asked riches, wealth, or honour, nor the life of thine enemies, neither yet hast asked long life; but hast asked wisdom and knowledge for thyself, that thou mayest judge my people, over whom I have made thee king: wisdom and knowledge is granted unto thee; and I will give thee riches, and wealth, and honour" (2Chronicles 1:11, 12).

Knowledge Of God And Christ

"I will set him on high, because he hath known my name" (Psalm 91:14).

"And this is life eternal, that they might know thee the only true God, and Jesus Christ, whom thou hast sent" (John 17:3).

"Grace and peace be multiplied unto you through the knowledge of God, and of Jesus our Lord, According as his divine power hath given unto us all things that pertain unto life and godliness, through the knowledge of him that hath called us to glory and virtue" (2Peter 1:2, 3).

Learning Of Christ

"Take my yoke upon you, and learn of me; for I am meek and lowly in heart: and ye shall find rest unto your souls" (Matthew 11:29).

10. To A Due Regard To The Word Of God

To Hearing And Reading The Word

"Blessed is the man that heareth me, watching daily at my gates, waiting at the posts of my doors" (Proverbs 8:34).

"Come ye, and let us go up to the mountain of the LORD, to the house of the God of Jacob; and he will teach us of his ways, and we will walk in his paths" (Isaiah 2:3).

"It pleased God by the foolishness of preaching to save them that believe" (1Corinthians 1:21).

"Search the Scriptures; for in them ye think ye have eternal life: and they are they which testify of me" (John 5:39).

"Unto you that hear shall more be given. For he that hath, to him shall be given: and he that hath not, from him shall be taken even that which he hath" (Mark 4:24, 25).

"Hearken diligently unto me, and eat ye that which is good, and let your soul delight itself in fatness. Incline your ear, and come unto me: hear, and your soul shall live; and I will make an everlasting covenant with you, even the sure mercies of David. For as the rain cometh down, and the snow from heaven, and returneth not thither, but watereth the earth, and maketh it bring forth and bud, that it may give seed to the sower, and bread to the eater: so shall my word be that goeth forth out of my mouth: it shall not return unto me void, but it shall accomplish that which I please, and it shall prosper in the thing whereto I sent it. For ye shall go out with joy, and be led forth with peace" (Isaiah 55:2, 3, 10-12).

"Faith cometh by hearing, and hearing by the word of God" (Romans 10:17).

"Blessed is he that readeth, and they that hear the words of this prophecy, and keep those things which are written therein" (Revelation 1:3).

"I am not ashamed of the gospel of Christ: for it is the power of God unto salvation to every one that believeth" (Romans 1:16).

"Wherefore lay apart all filthiness and superfluity of naughtiness, and receive with meekness the engrafted word, which is able to save your souls" (James 1:21).

"We have also a more sure word of prophecy; whereunto ye do well that ye take heed, as unto a light that shineth in a dark place, until the day dawn, and the day star arise in your hearts" (2Peter 1:19).

"The law of the LORD is perfect, converting the soul: the testimony of the LORD is sure, making wise the simple. The statutes of the LORD are right, rejoicing the heart: the commandment of the LORD is pure, enlightening the eyes. Moreover by them is thy servant warned: and in keeping of them there is great reward" (Psalm 19:7, 8, 11).

"The commandment is a lamp; and the law is light; and reproofs of instruction are the way of life" (Proverbs 6:23).

"The holy Scriptures, which are able to make thee wise unto salvation through faith which is in Christ Jesus" (2Timothy 3:15).

"Thy word is a lamp unto my feet, and a light unto my path. The entrance of thy words giveth light; it giveth understanding unto the simple" (Psalm 119:105).

"For the word of God is quick, and powerful, and sharper than any twoedged sword, piercing even to the dividing asunder of soul and spirit, and of the joints and marrow, and is a discerner of the thoughts and intents of the heart" (Hebrews 4:12).

Loving The Word

"Great peace have they which love thy law: and nothing shall offend them" (Psalm 119:165).

"As newborn babes, desire the sincere milk of the word, that ye may grow thereby" (1Peter 2:2).

"Blessed is the man that feareth the LORD, that delighteth greatly in his commandments" (Psalm 112:1).

Trembling At The Word

"He that feareth the commandment shall be rewarded" (Proverbs 13:13).

"To this man will I look, even to him that is poor and of a contrite spirit, and trembleth at my word" (Isaiah 66:2).

11. Meditation

"Mercy and truth shall be to them that devise good" (Proverbs 14:22).

"The law of his God is in his heart; none of his steps shall slide" (Psalm 37:31).

"This book of the law shall not depart out of thy mouth; but thou shalt meditate therein day and night, that thou mayest observe to do according to all that is written therein: for then thou shalt make thy way prosperous, and then thou shalt have good success" (Joshua 1:8).

"Therefore shall ye lay up these my words in your heart and in your soul, and bind them for a sign upon your hand, that they may be as frontlets between your eyes; that your days may be multiplied, and the days of your children, in the land which the LORD sware unto your fathers to give them, as the days of heaven upon the earth" (Deuteronomy 11:18, 21).

"Wherewithal shall a young man cleanse his way? by taking heed thereto according to thy word" (Psalm 119:9).

"Thou meetest him that rejoiceth and worketh righteousness, those that remember thee in thy ways" (Isaiah 64:5).

"Ponder the path of thy feet, and let all thy ways be established [or, all thy ways shall be ordered aright]" (Proverbs 4:26).

"5 My soul shall be satisfied as with marrow and fatness; and my mouth shall praise thee with joyful lips: when I remember thee upon my bed, and meditate on thee in the night watches" (Psalm 63:5, 6).

"The mercy of the LORD is from everlasting to everlasting upon them that fear him, and his righteousness unto children's children; to such as keep his covenant, and to those that remember his commandments to do them" (Psalm 103:17, 18).

"His delight is in the law of the LORD; and in his law doth he meditate day and night. And he shall be like a tree planted by the rivers of water, that bringeth forth his fruit in his season; his leaf also shall not wither; and whatsoever he doeth shall prosper" (Psalm 1:2, 3).

12. To Fasting

"Blow the trumpet in Zion, sanctify a fast, call a solemn assembly: gather the people, sanctify the congregation, assemble the elders, gather the children, and those that suck the breasts: let the bridegroom go forth of his chamber, and the bride out of her closet. let the priests, the ministers of the LORD, weep between the porch and the altar, and let them say, Spare thy people, O LORD, and give not thine heritage to reproach, that the heathen should rule over them: wherefore should they say among the people, Where is their God? Then will the LORD be jealous for his land, and pity his people" (Joel 2:15-18).

Fasting In Secret

"Thou, when thou fastest, anoint thine head, and wash thy face; 18 That thou appear not unto men to fast, but unto thy Father which is in secret: and thy Father, which seeth in secret, shall reward thee openly" (Matthew 6:17, 18).

13. To Baptism

"He that believeth and is baptized shall be saved" (Mark 16:16).

"Repent, and be baptized every one of you in the name of Jesus Christ for the remission of sins, and ye shall receive the gift of the Holy Ghost" (Acts 2:38).

"For as many of you as have been baptized into Christ have put on Christ" (Galatians 3:27).

"Arise, and be baptized, and wash away thy sins, calling on the name of the Lord" (Acts 22:16).

"By one Spirit are we all baptized into one body, whether we be Jews or Gentiles, whether we be bond or free" (1Corinthians 12:13).

"Buried with him in baptism, wherein also ye are risen with him through the faith of the operation of God, who hath raised him from the dead" (Colossians 2:12).

"Wherein [that is, in the ark] few, that is, eight souls were saved by water. The like figure whereunto even baptism doth also now save us (not the putting away of the filth of the flesh, but the answer of a good conscience toward God,) by the resurrection of Jesus Christ" (1Peter 3:20, 21).

"Know ye not, that so many of us as were baptized into Jesus Christ were baptized into his death? Therefore we are buried with him by baptism into death: that like as Christ was raised up from the dead by the glory of the Father, even so we also should walk in newness of life" (Romans 6:3, 4).

14. To The Lord's Supper

"[We] have been all made to drink into one Spirit" (1Corinthians 12:13).

"The cup of blessing which we bless, is it not the communion of the blood of Christ? The bread which we break, is it not the communion of the body of Christ?" (1Corinthians 10:16).

"Jesus took bread, and blessed it, and brake it, and gave it to the disciples, and said, Take, eat; this is my body. And he took the cup, and gave thanks, and gave it to them, saying, Drink ye all of it; for this is my blood of the new testament, which is shed for many for the remission of sins" (Matthew 26:26-28).

"Whoso eateth my flesh, and drinketh my blood, hath eternal life; and I will raise him up at the last day. For my flesh is meat indeed, and my blood is drink indeed. He that eateth my flesh, and drinketh my blood, dwelleth in me, and I in him. As the living Father hath sent me, and I live by the Father: so he that eateth me, even he shall live by me. It is the spirit that quickeneth; the flesh profiteth nothing: the words that I speak unto you, they are spirit, and they are life" (John 6:54-57, 63).

"Eat, O friends; drink, yea, drink abundantly, O beloved" (Song of Solomon 5:1).

"I sat down under his shadow with great delight, and his fruit was sweet to my taste. He brought me to the banqueting house, and his banner over me was love" (Song of Solomon 2:3, 4).

"And in this mountain shall the LORD of hosts make unto all

people a feast of fat things, a feast of wines on the lees, of fat things full of marrow, of wines on the lees well refined" (Isaiah 25:6).

15. To Good Discourse

"A wholesome tongue is a tree of life. A man hath joy by the answer of his mouth: and a word spoken in due season, how good is it!" (Proverbs 15:4, 23).

"Then they that feared the LORD spake often one to another: and the LORD hearkened, and heard it, and a book of remembrance was written before him for them that feared the LORD, and that thought upon his name. And they shall be mine, saith the LORD of hosts, in that day when I make up my jewels; and I will spare them, as a man spareth his own son that serveth him" (Malachi 3:16, 17).

"A man shall eat good by the fruit of his mouth" (Proverbs 13:2).

"Pleasant words are as an honeycomb, sweet to the soul, and health to the bones" (Proverbs 16:24).

"A man's belly shall be satisfied with the fruit of his mouth; and with the increase of his lips shall he be filled. Death and life are in the power of the tongue: and they that love it shall eat the fruit thereof" (Proverbs 18:20, 21).

"The mouth of the upright shall deliver them. A man shall be satisfied with good by the fruit of his mouth: and the recompence of a man's hands shall be rendered unto him. The tongue of the wise is health" (Proverbs 12:6, 14, 18).

The Government Of The Tongue

"The lips of the wise shall preserve them" (Proverbs 14:3).

"Whoso keepeth his mouth and his tongue keepeth his soul from troubles" (Proverbs 21:23).

"He that will love life, and see good days, let him refrain his tongue from evil, and his lips that they speak no guile" (1Peter 3:10).

"He that keepeth his mouth keepeth his life" (Proverbs 13:3).

"By thy words thou shalt be justified, and by thy words thou shalt be condemned" (Matthew 12:37).

16. To Watchfulness

"Wherefore let him that thinketh he standeth take heed lest he fall" (1Corinthians 10:12).

"Happy is the man that feareth alway: but he that hardeneth his heart shall fall into mischief" (Proverbs 28:14).

"Watch ye therefore, lest coming suddenly he find you sleeping, and what I say unto you I say unto all, Watch" (Mark 13:35, 36, 37).

"Behold, I come as a thief. Blessed is he that watcheth, and keepeth his garments, lest he walk naked, and they see his shame" (Revelation 16:15).

"Blessed are those servants, whom the Lord when he cometh shall find watching... and will come forth and serve them. And if he shall come in the second watch, or come in the third watch, and find them so, blessed are those servants" (Luke 12:37, 38).

17. To Keeping Good Company

"Iron sharpeneth iron; so a man sharpeneth the countenance of his friend" (Proverbs 27:17).

"He that walketh with wise men shall be wise: but a companion of fools shall be destroyed" (Proverbs 13:20).

Avoiding Evil Company

"Blessed is the man that walketh not in the counsel of the ungodly, nor standeth in the way of sinners, nor sitteth in the seat of the scornful" (Psalm 1:1).

"Come out from among them, and be ye separate, saith the Lord, and touch not the unclean thing; and I will receive you" (2Corinthians 6:17).

18. To Performing Oaths

"LORD, who shall abide in thy tabernacle? who shall dwell in thy holy hill? He that sweareth to his own hurt, and changeth not" (Psalm 15:1, 4).

"[He] who hath not lifted up his soul unto vanity, nor sworn deceitfully; he shall receive the blessing from the LORD, and righteousness from the God of his salvation" (Psalm 24:4, 5).

19. To The Keeping Of The Sabbath

"The LORD blessed the Sabbath day, and hallowed it" (Exodus 20:11).

"If thou turn away thy foot from the Sabbath, from doing thy pleasure on my holy day; and call the Sabbath a delight, the holy of the LORD, honourable; and shalt honour him, not doing thine own ways, nor finding thine own pleasure, nor speaking thine own words: then shalt thou delight thyself in the LORD; and I will cause thee to ride upon the high places of the earth, and feed thee with the heritage of Jacob thy father: for the mouth of the LORD hath spoken it" (Isaiah 58:13, 14).

"Blessed is the man that doeth this, and the son of man that layeth hold on it; that keepeth the Sabbath from polluting it, and keepeth his hand from doing any evil. The sons of the stranger, that join themselves to the LORD, to serve him, and to love the name of the LORD, to be his servants, every one that keepeth the Sabbath from polluting it, and taketh hold of my covenant; even them will I bring to my holy mountain, and make them joyful in my house of prayer: their burnt offerings and their sacrifices shall be accepted upon mine altar; for mine house shall be called an house of prayer for all people" (Isaiah 56:2, 6, 7).

"The Sabbath was made for man, and not man for the Sabbath" (Mark 2:27).

"This is the day which the LORD hath made; we will rejoice and be glad in it" (Psalm 118:24).

"Upon the first day of the week, when the disciples came together to break bread, Paul preached unto them" (Acts 20:7).

"Hallow my Sabbaths; and they shall be a sign between me and you, that ye may know that I am the LORD your God" (Ezekiel 20:20).

"The same day at evening, being the first day of the week... came Jesus and stood in the midst, and saith unto them, Peace be unto you" (John 20:19).

"I was in the Spirit on the Lord's day, and heard behind me a great voice, as of a trumpet, saying, I am Alpha and Omega, the first and the last" (Revelation 1:10, 11).

"It shall come to pass, if ye diligently hearken unto me, saith the LORD, to... hallow the Sabbath day, to do no work therein; then shall there enter into the gates of this city kings and princes sitting upon the throne of David" (Jeremiah 17:24, 25).

Chapter 2

In The Performance Of Duty Toward Men

1. To Obedience To Parents

"Children, obey your parents in the Lord: for this is right. Honour thy father and mother; (which is the first commandment with promise;) that it may be well with thee, and thou mayest live long on the earth" (Ephesians 6:1-3).

"My son, hear the instruction of thy father, and forsake not the law of thy mother: for they shall be an ornament of grace unto thy head, and chains about thy neck" (Proverbs 1:8, 9).

"But if any widow have children or nephews [grandchildren], let them learn first to shew piety at home, and to requite their parents: for that is good and acceptable before God" (1Timothy 5:4).

"Children, obey your parents in all things: for this is well pleasing unto the Lord" (Colossians 3:20).

"My son, keep thy father's commandment, and forsake not the law of thy mother: bind them continually upon thine heart, and tie them about thy neck. When thou goest, it shall lead thee; when thou sleepest, it shall keep thee; and when thou awakest, it shall talk with thee" (Proverbs 6:20-22).

"Thus saith the LORD of hosts, the God of Israel; Because ye have obeyed the commandment of Jonadab your father, and kept all his precepts, and done according unto all that he hath commanded you: therefore thus saith the LORD of hosts, the God of Israel; Jonadab the son of Rechab shall not want a man to stand before me for ever" (Jeremiah 35:18, 19).

2. To Good Education

"For I know him [Abraham], that he will command his children and his household after him, and they shall keep the way of the LORD, to do justice and judgment; that the LORD may bring upon Abraham that which he hath spoken of him" (Genesis 18:19).

"Train up a child in the way he should go: and when he is old, he will not depart from it" (Proverbs 22:6).

"And ye shall teach them your children, speaking of them when thou sittest in thine house, and when thou walkest by the way, when thou liest down, and when thou risest up. And thou shalt write them upon the door posts of thine house, and upon thy gates: that your days may be multiplied, and the days of your children, in the land which the LORD sware unto your fathers to give them, as the days of heaven upon the earth" (Deuteronomy 11:19-21).

Correction Of Children

"Foolishness is bound in the heart of a child; but the rod of correction shall drive it far from him" (Proverbs 22:15).

"Withhold not correction from the child: for if thou beatest him with the rod, he shall not die. Thou shalt beat him with the rod, and shalt deliver his soul from hell" (Proverbs 23:13, 14).

"The rod and reproof give wisdom: but a child left to himself bringeth his mother to shame. Correct thy son, and he shall give thee rest; yea, he shall give delight unto thy soul" (Proverbs 29:15, 17).

3. To A Good Wife

"Every wise woman buildeth her house" (Proverbs 14:1).

"A gracious woman retaineth honour: and strong men retain riches" (Proverbs 11:16).

"A virtuous woman is a crown to her husband: but she that maketh ashamed is as rottenness in his bones" (Proverbs 12:4).

"Who can find a virtuous woman? for her price is far above rubies. Strength and honour are her clothing; and she shall rejoice in time to come. Her children arise up, and call her blessed; her husband also, and he praiseth her. Favour is deceitful, and beauty is vain: but a woman that feareth the LORD, she shall be praised. Give her of the fruit of her hands; and let her own works praise her in the gates" (Proverbs 31:10, 25, 28, 30, 31).

4. To Faithful Servants

"Whoso keepeth the fig tree shall eat the fruit thereof: so he that waiteth on his master shall be honoured" (Proverbs 27:18).

"A wise servant shall have rule over a son that causeth shame, and shall have part of the inheritance among the brethren" (Proverbs 17:2).

"The king's favour is toward a wise servant" (Proverbs 14:35).

"Servants, obey in all things your masters according to the flesh; not with eyeservice, as menpleasers; but in singleness of heart, fearing God: knowing that of the Lord ye shall receive the reward of the inheritance: for ye serve the Lord Christ" (Colossians 3:22, 24).

"Servants, be obedient to them that are your masters according to the flesh, with fear and trembling, in singleness of your heart, as unto Christ; not with eyeservice, as menpleasers; but as the servants of Christ, doing the will of God from the heart; with good will doing service, as to the Lord, and not to men: knowing that whatsoever good thing any man doeth, the same shall he receive of the Lord, whether he be bond or free" (Ephesians 6:5-8).

5. To Good Kings And Magistrates

"The throne is established by righteousness" (Proverbs 16:12).

"Mercy and truth preserve the king: and his throne is upholden by mercy" (Proverbs 20:28).

"The king that faithfully judgeth the poor, his throne shall be established for ever" (Proverbs 29:14).

"In that day shall the LORD of hosts be... for a spirit of judgment to him that sitteth in judgment, and for strength to them that turn the battle to the gate" (Isaiah 28:5, 6).

"And it shall be, when he sitteth upon the throne of his kingdom, that he shall write him a copy of this law in a book out of that which is before the priests the Levites: and it shall be with him, and he shall read therein all the days of his life: that he may learn to fear the LORD his God, to keep all the words of this law and these statutes, to do them: that his heart be not lifted up above his brethren, and that he turn not aside from the commandment, to the right hand, or to the left: to the end that he may prolong his days in his kingdom, he, and his children, in the midst of Israel" (Deuteronomy 17:18-20).

6. To Obedient Subjects

"Submit yourselves to every ordinance of man for the Lord's sake: whether it be to the king, as supreme; or unto governors, as unto them that are sent by him for the punishment of evildoers, and for the praise of them that do well. For so is the will of God, that with well doing ye may put to silence the ignorance of foolish men" (1Peter 2:13-15).

"Whoso keepeth the commandment [the king's] shall feel no evil thing: and a wise man's heart discerneth both time and judgment" (Ecclesiastes 8:5).

7. To Faithful Ministers

"Then I said, I have laboured in vain, I have spent my strength for nought, and in vain: yet surely my judgment is with the LORD, and my work with my God" (Isaiah 49:4).

"Blessed are ye that sow beside all waters, that send forth thither the feet of the ox and the ass" (Isaiah 32:20).

"And I will satiate the soul of the priests with fatness, and my people shall be satisfied with my goodness, saith the LORD" (Jeremiah 31:14).

"The elders which are among you I exhort... feed the flock of God which is among you, taking the oversight thereof, not by constraint, but willingly; not for filthy lucre, but of a ready mind; Neither as being lords over God's heritage, but being ensamples to the flock. And when the chief Shepherd shall appear, ye shall receive a crown of glory that fadeth not away" (1Peter 5:1-4).

"These things saith he that holdeth the seven stars in his right hand" (Revelation 2:1).

"Take heed unto thyself, and unto the doctrine; continue in them: for in doing this thou shalt both save thyself, and them that hear thee" (1Timothy 4:16).

"And they that be wise shall shine as the brightness of the firmament; and they that turn many to righteousness as the stars for ever and ever" (Daniel 12:3).

"Teaching them to observe all things whatsoever I have commanded you: and, lo, I am with you alway, even unto the end of the world" (Matthew 28:20).

"And he that reapeth receiveth wages, and gathereth fruit unto life eternal: that both he that soweth and he that reapeth may rejoice together" (John 4:36).

"Who then is that faithful and wise steward, whom his lord shall make ruler over his household, to give them their portion of meat in due season? Blessed is that servant, whom his lord when he cometh shall find so doing. Of a truth I say unto you, that he will make him ruler over all that he hath" (Luke 12:42-44).

"I will also clothe her priests with salvation: and her saints shall shout aloud for joy" (Psalm 132:16).

"The LORD is with me as a mighty terrible one: therefore my persecutors shall stumble, and they shall not prevail: they shall be greatly ashamed; for they shall not prosper: their everlasting confusion shall never be forgotten" (Jeremiah 20:11).

"Behold, I have made thy face strong against their faces, and thy forehead strong against their foreheads. As an adamant harder than flint have I made thy forehead: fear them not, neither be dismayed at their looks, though they be a rebellious house" (Ezekiel 3:8, 9).

"Thus saith the LORD, If thou return, then will I bring thee again, and thou shalt stand before me: and if thou take forth the precious from the vile, thou shalt be as my mouth: let them return unto thee; but return not thou unto them. And I will make thee unto this people a fenced brasen wall: and they shall fight against thee, but they shall not prevail against thee: for I am with thee to save thee and to deliver thee, saith the LORD. And I will deliver thee out of the hand of the wicked, and I will redeem thee out of the hand of the terrible" (Jeremiah 15:19-21).

"I will give you a mouth and wisdom, which all your adversaries shall not be able to gainsay nor resist" (Luke 21:15).

"Levi hath no part nor inheritance with his brethren; the LORD is his inheritance, according as the LORD thy God promised him" (Deuteronomy 10:9).

"Bless, LORD, his substance [Levi's], and accept the work of his hands: smite through the loins of them that rise against him, and of them that hate him, that they rise not again" (Deuteronomy 33:11).

"When they deliver you up, take no thought how or what ye shall speak: for it shall be given you in that same hour what ye shall speak. For it is not ye that speak, but the Spirit of your Father which speaketh in you" (Matthew 10:19, 20).

"The LORD said unto me, Say not, I am a child: for thou shalt go to all that I shall send thee, and whatsoever I command thee thou shalt speak. Be not afraid of their faces: for I am with thee to deliver thee, saith the LORD. They shall fight against thee; but they shall not prevail against thee; for I am with thee, saith the LORD, to deliver thee" (Jeremiah 1:7, 8, 19).

8. To Them That Receive And Hearken To Ministers

"He that heareth you heareth me" (Luke 10:16).

"Believe in the LORD your God, so shall ye be established; believe his prophets, so shall ye prosper" (2Chronicles 20:20).

"He that receiveth you receiveth me, and he that receiveth me receiveth him that sent me. [See John 13:20]. He that receiveth a prophet in the name of a prophet shall receive a prophet's reward; and he that receiveth a righteous man in the name of a righteous man shall receive a righteous man's reward" (Matthew 10:40, 41).

9. To Love And Unity

"By this shall all men know that ye are my disciples, if ye have love one to another" (John 13:35).

"He that loveth his brother abideth in the light, and there is none occasion of stumbling in him" (1John 2:10).

"Be perfect, be of good comfort, be of one mind, live in peace; and the God of love and peace shall be with you" (2Corinthians 13:11).

"Behold, how good and how pleasant it is for brethren to dwell together in unity! It is like the precious ointment upon the head, that ran down upon the beard, even Aaron's beard: that went down to the skirts of his garments; As the dew of Hermon, and as the dew that descended upon the mountains of Zion: for there the LORD commanded the blessing, even life for evermore" (Psalm 133:1-3).

To The Peacemakers

"To the counsellors of peace is joy" (Proverbs 12:20).

"Blessed are the peacemakers: for they shall be called the children of God" (Matthew 5:9).

"He that will love life, and see good days... let him seek peace, and ensue it" (1Peter 3:10, 11).

Love To God's People

"Pray for the peace of Jerusalem: they shall prosper that love thee" (Psalm 122:6).

"LORD, who shall abide in thy tabernacle? who shall dwell in thy holy hill? [He] in whose eyes a vile person is contemned; but he honoureth them that fear the LORD" (Psalm 15:1, 4).

"If we love one another, God dwelleth in us, and his love is perfected in us" (1John 4:12).

"Blessed is he that blesseth thee, and cursed is he that curseth thee" (Numbers 24:9).

"God is not unrighteous to forget your work and labour of love, which ye have shewed toward his name, in that ye have ministered to the saints, and do minister" (Hebrews 6:10).

"We know that we have passed from death unto life, because we love the brethren. He that loveth not his brother abideth in death. My little children, let us not love in word, neither in tongue; but in deed and in truth. And hereby we know that we are of the truth, and shall assure our hearts before him" (1John 3:14, 18, 19).

10. To The Charitable, The Merciful, And The Liberal To God's Ministers

"He that hath mercy on the poor, happy is he" (Proverbs 14:21).

"He that hath pity upon the poor lendeth unto the LORD; and that which he hath given will he pay him again" (Proverbs 19:17).

"I have been young, and now am old; yet have I not seen the righteous forsaken, nor his seed begging bread. He is ever merciful, and lendeth; and his seed is blessed" (Psalm 37:25, 26).

"There is that scattereth, and yet increaseth; and there is that withholdeth more than is meet, but it tendeth to poverty. The liberal soul shall be made fat: and he that watereth shall be watered also himself. He that diligently seeketh good procureth favour" (Proverbs 11:24, 25, 27).

"A good man sheweth favour, and lendeth: he will guide his affairs with discretion. Surely he shall not be moved for ever: the righteous shall be in everlasting remembrance. He hath dispersed, he hath given to the poor; his righteousness endureth for ever; his horn shall be exalted with honour" (Psalm 112:5, 6, 9).

"Blessed is he that considereth the poor: the LORD will deliver him in time of trouble. The LORD will preserve him, and keep him alive; and he shall be blessed upon the earth: and thou wilt not deliver him unto the will of his enemies. The LORD will strengthen him upon the bed of languishing: thou wilt make all his bed in his sickness" (Psalm 41:1-3).

"And whosoever shall give to drink unto one of these little ones a cup of cold water only in the name of a disciple, verily I say unto you, he shall in no wise lose his reward" (Matthew 10:42).

"Cast thy bread upon the waters: for thou shalt find it after many days. Give a portion to seven, and also to eight; for thou knowest not what evil shall be upon the earth" (Ecclesiastes 11:1, 2).

"Is it not [the fast that I have chosen] to deal thy bread to the hungry, and that thou bring the poor that are cast out to thy house? When thou seest the naked, that thou cover him; and that thou hide not thyself from thine own flesh? Then shall thy light break forth as the morning, and thine health shall spring forth speedily: and thy righteousness shall go before thee; the glory of the LORD shall be thy rereward. If thou draw out thy soul to the hungry, and satisfy the afflicted soul; then shall thy light rise in obscurity, and thy darkness be as the noonday: and the LORD shall guide thee continually, and satisfy thy soul in drought, and make fat thy bones: and thou shalt be like a watered garden, and like a spring of water, whose waters fail not" (Isaiah 58:7, 8, 10, 11).

"The liberal deviseth liberal things; and by liberal things shall he stand" (Isaiah 32:8).

"He that hath a bountiful eye shall be blessed; for he giveth of his bread to the poor" (Proverbs 22:9).

"He that by usury and unjust gain increaseth his substance, he shall gather it for him that will pity the poor. He that giveth unto the poor shall not lack" (Proverbs 28:8, 27).

"And I say unto you, Make to yourselves friends of the mammon of unrighteousness; that, when ye fail, they may receive you into everlasting habitations" (Luke 16:9).

"Then shall the King say unto them on his right hand, Come, ye blessed of my Father, inherit the kingdom prepared for you from the foundation of the world: for I was an hungred, and ye gave me meat: I was thirsty, and ye gave me drink: I was a stranger, and ye took me in: naked, and ye clothed me: I was sick, and ye visited me: I was in prison, and ye came unto me. Verily I say unto you, Inasmuch as ye have done it unto one of the least of these my brethren, ye have done it unto me" (Matthew 25:34-36, 40).

"Give alms of such things as ye have; and, behold, all things are clean unto you" (Luke 11:41).

"Sell that ye have, and give alms; provide yourselves bags which wax not old, a treasure in the heavens that faileth not, where no thief approacheth, neither moth corrupteth" (Luke 12:33).

"When thou makest a feast, call the poor, the maimed, the lame, the blind: and thou shalt be blessed; for they cannot recompense thee: for thou shalt be recompensed at the resurrection of the just" (Luke 14:13, 14).

"Give, and it shall be given unto you; good measure, pressed down, and shaken together, and running over, shall men give into your bosom. For with the same measure that ye mete withal it shall be measured to you again" (Luke 6:38).

"God is able to make all grace abound toward you; that ye, always having all sufficiency in all things, may abound to every good work: Now he that ministereth seed to the sower both minister bread for your food, and multiply your seed sown, and increase the fruits of your righteousness" (2Corinthians 9:8, 10).

"To do good and to communicate forget not: for with such sacrifices God is well pleased" (Hebrews 13:16).

"Go thy way, sell whatsoever thou hast, and give to the poor, and thou shalt have treasure in heaven" (Mark 10:21).

"If there be first a willing mind, it is accepted according to that a man hath, and not according to that he hath not" (2Corinthians 8:12).

"He which soweth sparingly shall reap also sparingly; and he which soweth bountifully shall reap also bountifully. God loveth a cheerful giver" (2Corinthians 9:6, 7).

"Thou shalt surely give him [thy poor brother], and thine heart shall not be grieved when thou givest unto him: because that for this thing the LORD thy God shall bless thee in all thy works, and in all that thou puttest thine hand unto" (Deuteronomy 15:10).

"Charge them that are rich in this world, that they do good, that they be rich in good works, ready to distribute, willing to communicate; laying up in store for themselves a good foundation against the time to come, that they may lay hold on eternal life" (1Timothy 6:17-19).

To Alms In Secret

"When thou doest alms, let not thy left hand know what thy right hand doeth: that thine alms may be in secret: and thy Father which seeth in secret himself shall reward thee openly" (Matthew 6:3, 4).

To The Supporting God's Ministers And Worship

"Honour the LORD with thy substance, and with the firstfruits of all thine increase: so shall thy barns be filled with plenty, and thy presses shall burst out with new wine" (Proverbs 3:9, 10).

"And the Levite, (because he hath no part nor inheritance with thee,) and the stranger, and the fatherless, and the widow, which are within thy gates, shall come, and shall eat and be satisfied; that the LORD thy God may bless thee in all the work of thine hand which thou doest" (Deuteronomy 14:29).

"Bring ye all the tithes into the storehouse, that there may be meat in mine house, and prove me now herewith, saith the LORD of hosts, if I will not open you the windows of heaven, and pour you out a blessing, that there shall not be room enough to receive it. And I will rebuke the devourer for your sakes, and he shall not destroy the fruits of your ground; neither shall your vine cast her fruit before the time in the field, saith the LORD of hosts. And all nations shall call you blessed: for ye shall be a delightsome land, saith the LORD of hosts" (Malachi 3:10-12).

"Let him that is taught in the word communicate unto him that teacheth in all good things. Be not deceived; God is not mocked: for whatsoever a man soweth, that shall he also reap. For he that soweth to his flesh shall of the flesh reap corruption; but he that soweth to the Spirit shall of the Spirit reap life everlasting" (Galatians 6:6-8).

"Not because I desire a gift: but I desire fruit that may abound to your account. But I have all, and abound: I am full, having received of Epaphroditus the things which were sent from you, an odour of a sweet smell, a sacrifice acceptable, wellpleasing to God. But my God shall supply all your need according to his riches in glory by Christ Jesus" (Philippians 4:17-19).

To The Merciful

"The merciful man doeth good to his own soul: but he that is cruel troubleth his own flesh" (Proverbs 11:17).

"Blessed are the merciful: for they shall obtain mercy" (Matthew 5:7).

"With the merciful thou wilt shew thyself merciful" (Psalm 18:25).

"Let not mercy and truth forsake thee: bind them about thy neck; write them upon the table of thine heart: So shalt thou find favour and good understanding in the sight of God and man" (Proverbs 3:3, 4).

"If the man be poor, thou shalt not sleep with his pledge: In any case thou shalt deliver him the pledge again when the sun goeth down, that he may sleep in his own raiment, and bless thee: and it shall be righteousness unto thee before the LORD thy God" (Deuteronomy 24:12, 13).

11. To The Giving And Receiving Of Reproofs

"To them that rebuke him shall be delight, and a good blessing shall come upon them" (Proverbs 24:25).

"He that rebuketh a man afterwards shall find more favour than he that flattereth with the tongue" (Proverbs 28:23).

"Poverty and shame shall be to him that refuseth instruction: but he that regardeth reproof shall be honoured" (Proverbs 13:18).

"As an earring of gold, and an ornament of fine gold, so is a wise reprover upon an obedient ear" (Proverbs 25:12).

"The ear that heareth the reproof of life abideth among the wise. He that refuseth instruction despiseth his own soul: but he that heareth reproof getteth understanding" (Proverbs 15:31, 32).

12. To Forgiving Injuries

"Say not thou, I will recompense evil; but wait on the LORD, and he shall save thee" (Proverbs 20:22).

"Love ye your enemies, and do good, and lend, hoping for nothing again; and your reward shall be great, and ye shall be the children of the Highest: for he is kind unto the unthankful and to the evil. Forgive, and ye shall be forgiven" (Luke 6:35, 37).

"Love your enemies, bless them that curse you, do good to them that hate you, and pray for them which despitefully use you, and persecute you; that ye may be the children of your Father which is in heaven: for he maketh his sun to rise on the evil and on the good, and sendeth rain on the just and on the unjust" (Matthew 5:44, 45).

"If ye forgive men their trespasses, your heavenly Father will also forgive you" (Matthew 6:14).

"And when ye stand praying, forgive, if ye have ought against any: that your Father also which is in heaven may forgive you your trespasses" (Mark 11:25).

"Not rendering evil for evil, or railing for railing: but contrariwise blessing; knowing that ye are thereunto called, that ye should inherit a blessing" (1Peter 3:9).

"If thine enemy be hungry, give him bread to eat; and if he be thirsty, give him water to drink: for thou shalt heap coals of fire upon his head, and the LORD shall reward thee" (Proverbs 25:21, 22). See Rom. 12:20.

13. To Chastity And Purity

"Blessed are the pure in heart: for they shall see God" (Matthew 5:8).

"If a man be just, and do that which is lawful and right, and hath not eaten upon the mountains, neither hath lifted up his eyes to the idols of the house of Israel, neither hath defiled his neighbour's wife, neither hath come near to a menstruous woman, hath walked in my statutes, and hath kept my judgments, to deal truly; he is just, he shall surely live, saith the Lord GOD" (Ezekiel 18:5, 6, 9).

"Unto the pure all things are pure" (Titus 1:15).

"With the pure thou wilt shew thyself pure" (Psalm 18:26).

"Truly God is good to Israel, even to such as are of a clean heart"

(Psalm 73:1).

"Who shall ascend into the hill of the LORD? or who shall stand in his holy place? He that hath clean hands, and a pure heart" (Psalm 24:3, 4).

"If a man therefore purge himself from these, he shall be a vessel unto honour, sanctified, and meet for the master's use, and prepared unto every good work" (2Timothy 2:21).

14. To Diligence

"The hand of the diligent maketh rich" (Proverbs 10:4).

"In all labour there is profit: but the talk of the lips tendeth only to penury" (Proverbs 14:23).

"The soul of the sluggard desireth, and hath nothing: but the soul of the diligent shall be made fat. Wealth gotten by vanity shall be diminished: but he that gathereth by labour shall increase" (Proverbs 13:4, 11).

"The thoughts of the diligent tend only to plenteousness; but of every one that is hasty only to want" (Proverbs 21:5).

"Seest thou a man diligent in his business? he shall stand before kings; he shall not stand before mean men" (Proverbs 22:29).

"He that tilleth his land shall have plenty of bread: but he that followeth after vain persons shall have poverty enough" (Proverbs 28:19).

"He that tilleth his land shall be satisfied with bread. The hand of the diligent shall bear rule: but the slothful shall be under tribute. The substance of a diligent man is precious" (Proverbs 12:11, 24, 27).

To Improving Our Talents

"Well done, good and faithful servant; thou hast been faithful over a few things, I will make thee ruler over many things: enter thou into the joy of thy Lord. Unto every one that hath shall be given, and he shall have abundance" (Matthew 25:23, 29). See Matt. 13:12.

Moderation In Sleep

"Love not sleep, lest thou come to poverty; open thine eyes, and thou shalt be satisfied with bread" (Proverbs 20:13).

15. To The Just And Honest

"He that is greedy of gain troubleth his own house; but he that hateth gifts shall live" (Proverbs 15:27).

"A false balance is abomination to the LORD: but a just weight is his delight" (Proverbs 11:1).

"There shall no evil happen to the just: but the wicked shall be filled with mischief" (Proverbs 12:21).

"A faithful man shall abound with blessings: but he that maketh haste to be rich shall not be innocent" (Proverbs 28:20).

"That which is altogether just shalt thou follow, that thou mayest live, and inherit the land which the LORD thy God giveth thee" (Deuteronomy 16:20).

"He that walketh righteously, and speaketh uprightly; he that despiseth the gain of oppressions, that shaketh his hands from holding of bribes, that stoppeth his ears from hearing of blood, and shutteth his eyes from seeing evil; he shall dwell on high: his place of defence shall be the munitions of rocks: bread shall be given him; his waters shall be sure" (Isaiah 33:15, 16).

"Better is a little with righteousness than great revenues without right" (Proverbs 16:8).

"To do justice and judgment is more acceptable to the LORD than sacrifice" (Proverbs 21:3).

"He that putteth not out his money to usury, nor taketh reward against the innocent. He that doeth these things shall never be moved" (Psalm 15:5).

"Thou shalt have a perfect and just weight, a perfect and just measure shalt thou have: that thy days may be lengthened in the land which the LORD thy God giveth thee" (Deuteronomy 25:15).

"If a man be just, and do that which is lawful and right, and hath not oppressed any, but hath restored to the debtor his pledge, hath spoiled none by violence, hath given his bread to the hungry, and hath covered the naked with a garment; he that hath not given forth upon usury, neither hath taken any increase, that hath withdrawn his hand from iniquity, hath executed true judgment between man and man, hath walked in my statutes, and hath kept my judgments, to deal truly; he is just, he shall surely live, saith the Lord GOD" (Ezekiel 18:5, 7-9).

"Thus saith the LORD, Keep ye judgment, and do justice: for my salvation is near to come, and my righteousness to be revealed. Blessed is the man that doeth this, and the son of man that layeth hold on it" (Isaiah 56:1, 2).

16. To Truth

"He that will love life, and see good days, let him refrain his tongue from evil, and his lips that they speak no guile" (1Peter 3:10). See Psa. 34:12, 13.

"The lip of truth shall be established for ever: but a lying tongue is but for a moment. Lying lips are abomination to the LORD: but they that deal truly are his delight" (Proverbs 12:19, 22).

"LORD, who shall abide in thy tabernacle? who shall dwell in thy holy hill? [He that] speaketh the truth in his heart. He that backbiteth not with his tongue, nor doeth evil to his neighbour" (Psalm 15:1-3).

17. To Candor

"Judge not, that ye be not judged. 2 For with what judgment ye judge, ye shall be judged: and with what measure ye mete, it shall be measured to you again" (Matthew 7:1, 2).

"LORD, who shall abide in thy tabernacle? who shall dwell in thy holy hill? He that backbiteth not with his tongue, nor doeth evil to his neighbour, nor taketh up a reproach against his neighbour" (Psalm 15:1, 3).

18. To Contentment And Mortification

Contentment

"Godliness with contentment is great gain" (1Timothy 6:6).

"A sound heart is the life of the flesh: but envy the rottenness of the bones" (Proverbs 14:30).

"A merry heart doeth good like a medicine: but a broken spirit drieth the bones" (Proverbs 17:22).

"All the days of the afflicted are evil: but he that is of a merry heart hath a continual feast" (Proverbs 15:15).

"Let your conversation be without covetousness; and be content with such things as ye have: for he hath said, I will never leave thee, nor forsake thee" (Hebrews 13:5).

"Let not thine heart envy sinners: but be thou in the fear of the LORD all the day long. For surely there is an end; and thine expectation shall not be cut off" (Proverbs 23:17, 18).

Mortification Of Sin

"If ye through the Spirit do mortify the deeds of the body, ye shall live" (Romans 8:13).

"If thy right eye offend thee, pluck it out, and cast it from thee: for it is profitable for thee that one of thy members should perish, and not that thy whole body should be cast into hell. And if thy right hand offend thee, cut it off, and cast it from thee: for it is profitable for thee that one of thy members should perish, and not that thy whole body should be cast into hell" (Matthew 5:29, 30).

To The Spiritually-Minded

"To be carnally minded is death; but to be spiritually minded is life and peace" (Romans 8:6).

Chapter 3
In The Cultivation Of Christian Character

1. To The Meek, Humble, Contrite

The Meek

"Seek ye the LORD, all ye meek of the earth, which have wrought his judgment; seek righteousness, seek meekness: it may be ye shall be hid in the day of the LORD'S anger" (Zephaniah 2:3).

"A soft answer turneth away wrath: but grievous words stir up anger. He that is slow to anger appeaseth strife" (Proverbs 15:1, 18).

"Whose adorning let it not be that outward adorning of plaiting the hair, and of wearing of gold, or of putting on of apparel; but let it be the hidden man of the heart, in that which is not corruptible, even the ornament of a meek and quiet spirit, which is in the sight of God of great price" (1Peter 3:3, 4).

"He that is slow to wrath is of great understanding" (Proverbs 14:29).

"Blessed are the meek: for they shall inherit the earth" (Matthew 5:5).

"The meek will he guide in judgment: and the meek will he teach his way" (Psalm 25:9).

"The LORD lifteth up the meek: he casteth the wicked down to the ground" (Psalm 147:6).

"The LORD taketh pleasure in his people: he will beautify the meek with salvation" (Psalm 149:4).

"The meek shall inherit the earth; and shall delight themselves in the abundance of peace" (Psalm 37:11).

"With righteousness shall he judge the poor, and reprove with equity for the meek of the earth" (Isaiah 11:4).

"The meek shall eat and be satisfied: they shall praise the LORD that seek him: your heart shall live for ever" (Psalm 22:26).

"The meek also shall increase their joy in the LORD, and the poor among men shall rejoice in the Holy One of Israel" (Isaiah 29:19).

"It is an honour for a man to cease from strife" (Proverbs 20:3).

"The discretion of a man deferreth his anger; and it is his glory to pass over a transgression" (Proverbs 19:11).

"He that is slow to anger is better than the mighty; and he that ruleth his spirit than he that taketh a city" (Proverbs 16:32).

To The Humble

"He shall save the humble person" (Job 22:29).

"He forgetteth not the cry of the humble" (Psalm 9:12).

"LORD, thou hast heard the desire of the humble" (Psalm 10:17).

"Surely he scorneth the scorners: but he giveth grace unto the lowly" (Proverbs 3:34).

"When pride cometh, then cometh shame: but with the lowly is wisdom" (Proverbs 11:2).

"Wherefore he saith, God resisteth the proud, but giveth grace unto the humble" (James 4:6). See 1Peter 5:5.

"Though the LORD be high, yet hath he respect unto the lowly: but the proud he knoweth afar off" (Psalm 138:6).

"By humility and the fear of the LORD are riches, and honour, and life" (Proverbs 22:4).

"A man's pride shall bring him low: but honour shall uphold the humble in spirit" (Proverbs 29:23).

"The fear of the LORD is the instruction of wisdom; and before honour is humility" (Proverbs 15:33).

"Before destruction the heart of man is haughty, and before honour is humility" (Proverbs 18:12).

"Better it is to be of an humble spirit with the lowly, than to divide the spoil with the proud" (Proverbs 16:19).

"Whosoever therefore shall humble himself as this little child, the same is greatest in the kingdom of heaven" (Matthew 18:4).

"Whosoever shall exalt himself shall be abased; and he that shall humble himself shall be exalted" (Matthew 23:12). See Luke 18:14.

The Contrite And Mourners

"The LORD is nigh unto them that are of a broken heart; and saveth such as be of a contrite spirit" (Psalm 34:18).

"He healeth the broken in heart, and bindeth up their wounds" (Psalm 147:3).

"Sorrow is better than laughter: for by the sadness of the countenance the heart is made better" (Ecclesiastes 7:3).

"To this man will I look, even to him that is poor and of a contrite spirit, and trembleth at my word" (Isaiah 66:2).

"The sacrifices of God are a broken spirit: a broken and a contrite heart, O God, thou wilt not despise" (Psalm 51:17).

"Blessed are the poor in spirit: for theirs is the kingdom of heaven. 4 Blessed are they that mourn: for they shall be comforted" (Matthew 5:3, 4).

"Thus saith the high and lofty One that inhabiteth eternity, whose name is Holy; I dwell in the high and holy place, with him also that is of a contrite and humble spirit, to revive the spirit of the humble, and to revive the heart of the contrite ones" (Isaiah 57:15).

2. To Them That Suffer For Righteousness' Sake

"He that findeth his life shall lose it: and he that loseth his life for my sake shall find it" (Matthew 10:39).

"If we suffer, we shall also reign with him" (2Timothy 2:12).

"Every one that hath forsaken houses, or brethren, or sisters, or father, or mother, or wife, or children, or lands, for my name's sake, shall receive an hundredfold, and shall inherit everlasting life" (Matthew 19:29).

"Blessed are they which are persecuted for righteousness' sake: for theirs is the kingdom of heaven. Blessed are ye, when men shall revile you, and persecute you, and shall say all manner of evil against you falsely, for my sake. Rejoice, and be exceeding glad: for great is your reward in heaven: for so persecuted they the prophets which were before you" (Matthew 5:10-12).

"If so be that we suffer with him, that we may be also glorified together. Who shall separate us from the love of Christ? shall tribulation, or distress, or persecution, or famine, or nakedness, or peril, or sword? As it is written, For thy sake we are killed all the day long; we are accounted as sheep for the slaughter. Nay, in all these things we are more than conquerors through him that loved us" (Romans 8:17, 35-37).

"Persecuted, but not forsaken" (2Corinthians 4:9).

"If ye suffer for righteousness' sake, happy are ye: and be not afraid of their terror, neither be troubled; for it is better, if the will of God be so, that ye suffer for well doing, than for evil doing" (1Peter 3:14, 17).

"For ye had compassion of me in my bonds, and took joyfully the spoiling of your goods, knowing in yourselves that ye have in heaven a better and an enduring substance. Cast not away therefore your confidence, which hath great recompence of reward" (Hebrews 10:34, 35).

"Beloved, think it not strange concerning the fiery trial which is to try you, as though some strange thing happened unto you: but rejoice, inasmuch as ye are partakers of Christ's sufferings; that, when his glory shall be revealed, ye may be glad also with exceeding joy. If ye be reproached for the name of Christ, happy are ye; for the spirit of glory and of God resteth upon you: on their part he is evil spoken of, but on your part he is glorified" (1Peter 4:12-14).

To Them That Are Excommunicated Unjustly

"Hear the word of the LORD, ye that tremble at his word; Your brethren that hated you, that cast you out for my name's sake, said, Let the LORD be glorified: but he shall appear to your joy, and they shall be ashamed" (Isaiah 66:5).

"Blessed are ye, when men shall hate you, and when they shall separate you from their company, and shall reproach you, and cast out your name as evil, for the Son of man's sake. Rejoice ye in that day, and leap for joy: for, behold, your reward is great in heaven" (Luke 6:22, 23).

3. To Patience And Submission

"That ye be not slothful, but followers of them who through faith and patience inherit the promises" (Hebrews 6:12).

"26 It is good that a man should both hope and quietly wait for the salvation of the LORD. It is good for a man that he bear the yoke in his youth. He sitteth alone and keepeth silence, because he hath borne it upon him. He putteth his mouth in the dust; if so be there may be hope. For the Lord will not cast off for ever" (Lamentations 3:26-29, 31).

"The hope of the righteous shall be gladness" (Proverbs 10:28).

"We glory in tribulations also: knowing that tribulation worketh patience; and patience, experience; and experience, hope" (Romans 5:3, 4).

"My brethren, count it all joy when ye fall into divers temptations; knowing this, that the trying of your faith worketh patience. But let patience have her perfect work, that ye may be perfect and entire, wanting nothing. Blessed is the man that endureth temptation: for when he is tried, he shall receive the crown of life, which the Lord hath promised to them that love him" (James 1:2-4, 12).

"Be patient therefore, brethren, unto the coming of the Lord. Behold, the husbandman waiteth for the precious fruit of the earth, and hath long patience for it, until he receive the early and latter rain. Be ye also patient; stablish your hearts: for the coming of the Lord draweth nigh. Behold, we count them happy which endure. Ye have heard of the patience of Job, and have seen the end of the Lord; that the Lord is very pitiful, and of tender mercy" (James 5:7, 8, 11).

"Humble yourselves in the sight of the Lord, and he shall lift you up" (James 4:10).

"If, when ye do well, and suffer for it, ye take it patiently, this is acceptable with God" (1Peter 2:20).

"Humble yourselves therefore under the mighty hand of God, that he may exalt you in due time" (1Peter 5:6).

"Cast not away therefore your confidence, which hath great recompence of reward. For ye have need of patience, that, after ye have done the will of God, ye might receive the promise. For yet a little while, and he that shall come will come, and will not tarry" (Hebrews 10:35-37).

4. To Perseverance

"Let us not be weary in well doing: for in due season we shall reap, if we faint not" (Galatians 6:9).

"Look to yourselves, that we lose not those things which we have wrought, but that we receive a full reward. Whosoever transgresseth, and abideth not in the doctrine of Christ, hath not God. He that abideth in the doctrine of Christ, he hath both the Father and the Son" (2John 8, 9).

"He that endureth to the end shall be saved" (Matthew 10:22). See Matt. 24:13.

"Be thou faithful unto death, and I will give thee a crown of life" (Revelation 2:10).

"If ye continue in my word, then are ye my disciples indeed; and ye shall know the truth, and the truth shall make you free" (John 8:31, 32).

"My beloved brethren, be ye stedfast, unmoveable, always abounding in the work of the Lord, forasmuch as ye know that your labour is not in vain in the Lord" (1Corinthians 15:58).

"Let us hold fast the profession of our faith without wavering; for he is faithful that promised. Cast not away therefore your confidence, which hath great recompence of reward" (Hebrews 10:23, 35).

"Let that therefore abide in you, which ye have heard from the beginning. If that which ye have heard from the beginning shall remain in you, ye also shall continue in the Son, and in the Father. And now, little children, abide in him; that, when he shall appear, we may have confidence, and not be ashamed before him at his coming" (1John 2:24, 28).

"If ye abide in me, and my words abide in you, ye shall ask what ye will, and it shall be done unto you" (John 15:7).

To Him That Overcomes

"Be not overcome of evil, but overcome evil with good" (Romans 12:21).

"He that overcometh shall inherit all things; and I will be his God, and he shall be my son" (Revelation 21:7).

"To him that overcometh will I give to eat of the tree of life, which is in the midst of the paradise of God" (Revelation 2:7).

"He that overcometh, the same shall be clothed in white raiment; and I will not blot out his name out of the book of life, but I will confess his name before my Father, and before his angels. Him that overcometh will I make a pillar in the temple of my God, and he shall go no more out: and I will write upon him the name of my God, and the name of the city of my God, which is new Jerusalem, which cometh down out of heaven from my God: and I will write upon him my new name. To him that overcometh will I grant to sit with me in my throne, even as I also overcame, and am set down with my Father in his throne" (Revelation 3:5, 12, 21).

"He that overcometh shall not be hurt of the second death. To him that overcometh will I give to eat of the hidden manna, and will give him a white stone, and in the stone a new name written, which no man knoweth saving he that receiveth it. And he that overcometh, and keepeth my works unto the end, to him will I give power over the nations: And he shall rule them with a rod of iron; as the vessels of a potter shall they be broken to shivers: even as I received of my Father. 28 And I will give him the morning star" (Revelation 2:11, 17, 26-28).

PART THREE

Promises Of The Growth And Glory Of The Church

1. The Enlargement Of The Church, And Spread Of The Gospel, And Kingdom Of Christ

"Ask of me, and I shall give thee the heathen for thine inheritance, and the uttermost parts of the earth for thy possession. Thou shalt break them with a rod of iron; thou shalt dash them in pieces like a potter's vessel" (Psalm 2:8, 9).

"And the LORD shall be known to Egypt, and the Egyptians shall know the LORD in that day, and shall do sacrifice and oblation; yea, they shall vow a vow unto the LORD, and perform it. In that day shall Israel be the third with Egypt and with Assyria, even a blessing in the midst of the land: whom the LORD of hosts shall bless, saying, Blessed be Egypt my people, and Assyria the work of my hands, and Israel mine inheritance" (Isaiah 19:21, 24, 25).

"Princes shall come out of Egypt; Ethiopia shall soon stretch out her hands unto God" (Psalm 68:31).

"That thy way may be known upon earth, thy saving health among all nations. God shall bless us; and all the ends of the earth shall fear him" (Psalm 67:2, 7).

"He shall have dominion also from sea to sea, and from the river unto the ends of the earth. Yea, all kings shall fall down before him: all nations shall serve him. His name shall endure for ever: his name shall be continued as long as the sun: and men shall be blessed in him: all nations shall call him blessed. Let the whole earth be filled with his glory" (Psalm 72:8, 11, 17, 19).

"And it shall come to pass in the last days, that the mountain of the LORD'S house shall be established in the top of the mountains, and shall be exalted above the hills; and all nations shall flow unto it. And many people shall go and say, Come ye, and let us go up to the mountain of the LORD, to the house of the God of Jacob; and he will teach us of his ways, and we will walk in his paths: for out of Zion shall go forth the law, and the word of the LORD from Jerusalem" (Isaiah 2:2, 3). See Micah 4:2.

"All nations whom thou hast made shall come and worship before thee, O Lord; and shall glorify thy name" (Psalm 86:9).

"Thy people shall be willing in the day of thy power, in the beauties of holiness from the womb of the morning: thou hast the dew of thy youth" (Psalm 110:3).

"In that day there shall be a root of Jesse, which shall stand for an ensign of the people; to it shall the Gentiles seek: and his rest shall be glorious" (Isaiah 11:10).

"The heathen shall fear the name of the LORD, and all the kings of the earth thy glory. When the LORD shall build up Zion, he shall appear in his glory" (Psalm 102:15, 16).

"All the ends of the world shall remember and turn unto the

LORD: and all the kindreds of the nations shall worship before thee. For the kingdom is the LORD'S: and he is the governor among the nations" (Psalm 22:27, 28).

"And her [Tyre's] merchandise and her hire shall be holiness to the LORD: it shall not be treasured nor laid up; for her merchandise shall be for them that dwell before the LORD, to eat sufficiently, and for durable clothing" (Isaiah 23:18).

"He shall cause them that come of Jacob to take root: Israel shall blossom and bud, and fill the face of the world with fruit" (Isaiah 27:6).

"The voice of him that crieth in the wilderness, Prepare ye the way of the LORD, make straight in the desert a highway for our God. Every valley shall be exalted, and every mountain and hill shall be made low: and the crooked shall be made straight, and the rough places plain: And the glory of the LORD shall be revealed, and all flesh shall see it together: for the mouth of the LORD hath spoken it" (Isaiah 40:3-5).

"Behold my servant, whom I uphold; mine elect, in whom my soul delighteth; I have put my Spirit upon him: he shall bring forth judgment to the Gentiles. He shall not fail nor be discouraged, till he have set judgment in the earth: and the isles shall wait for his law. I the LORD have called thee in righteousness, and will hold thine hand, and will keep thee, and give thee for a covenant of the people, for a light of the Gentiles; to open the blind eyes, to bring out the prisoners from the prison, and them that sit in darkness out of the prison house" (Isaiah 42:1, 4, 6, 7).

"I have sworn by myself, the word is gone out of my mouth in righteousness, and shall not return, That unto me every knee shall bow, every tongue shall swear. Surely, shall one say, in the LORD have I righteousness and strength: even to him shall men come; and all that are incensed against him shall be ashamed" (Isaiah 45:23, 24). See verse 14.

"And he said, It is a light thing that thou shouldest be my servant to raise up the tribes of Jacob, and to restore the preserved of Israel: I will also give thee for a light to the Gentiles, that thou mayest be my salvation unto the end of the earth. Behold, these shall come from far: and, lo, these from the north and from the west; and these from the land of Sinim. Lift up thine eyes round about, and behold: all these gather themselves together, and come to thee. As I live, saith the LORD, thou shalt surely clothe thee with them all, as with an ornament, and bind them on thee, as a bride doeth. The children which thou shalt have, after thou hast lost the other, shall say again in thine ears, The place is too strait for me: give place to me that I may dwell" (Isaiah 49:6, 12, 18, 20). See verses 8, 9, 11, 19, 21, 22, and Chapter 60:4.

"The LORD hath made bare his holy arm in the eyes of all the nations; and all the ends of the earth shall see the salvation of our God" (Isaiah 52:10).

"The Gentiles shall come to thy light, and kings to the brightness of thy rising. Who are these that fly as a cloud, and as the doves to their windows? Surely the isles shall wait for me, and the ships of Tarshish first, to bring thy sons from far, their silver and their gold with them, unto the name of the LORD thy God, and to the Holy One of Israel, because he hath glorified thee. And the sons of strangers shall build up thy walls, and their kings shall minister unto thee: for in my wrath I smote thee, but in my favour have I had mercy on thee" (Isaiah 60:3, 8-10). See verses

4-7, 11, 16.

"Hearken unto me, my people; and give ear unto me, O my nation: for a law shall proceed from me, and I will make my judgment to rest for a light of the people. My righteousness is near; my salvation is gone forth, and mine arms shall judge the people; the isles shall wait upon me, and on mine arm shall they trust. I have put my words in thy mouth, and I have covered thee in the shadow of mine hand, that I may plant the heavens, and lay the foundations of the earth, and say unto Zion, Thou art my people" (Isaiah 51:4, 5, 16

"Behold, I have given him for a witness to the people, a leader and commander to the people. Behold, thou shalt call a nation that thou knowest not, and nations that knew not thee shall run unto thee because of the LORD thy God, and for the Holy One of Israel; for he hath glorified thee" (Isaiah 55:4, 5).

"So shall they fear the name of the LORD from the west, and his glory from the rising of the sun. When the enemy shall come in like a flood, the Spirit of the LORD shall lift up a standard against him. And the Redeemer shall come to Zion, and unto them that turn from transgression in Jacob, saith the LORD" (Isaiah 59:19, 20).

"Sing, O barren, thou that didst not bear; break forth into singing, and cry aloud, thou that didst not travail with child: for more are the children of the desolate than the children of the married wife, saith the LORD. Enlarge the place of thy tent, and let them stretch forth the curtains of thine habitations: spare not, lengthen thy cords, and strengthen thy stakes; for thou shalt break forth on the right hand and on the left; and thy seed shall inherit the Gentiles, and make the desolate cities to be inhabited"

(Isaiah 54:1-3).

"This gospel of the kingdom shall be preached in all the world for a witness unto all nations; and then shall the end come" (Matthew 24:14).

"Who hath heard such a thing? Who hath seen such things? Shall the earth be made to bring forth in one day? or shall a nation be born at once? For as soon as Zion travailed, she brought forth her children. Shall I bring to the birth, and not cause to bring forth? saith the LORD: shall I cause to bring forth, and shut the womb? saith thy God. It shall come, that I will gather all nations and tongues; and they shall come, and see my glory. And I will set a sign among them, and I will send those that escape of them unto the nations, to Tarshish, Pul, and Lud, that draw the bow, to Tubal, and Javan, to the isles afar off, that have not heard my fame, neither have seen my glory; and they shall declare my glory among the Gentiles. And they shall bring all your brethren for an offering unto the LORD out of all nations. And it shall come to pass, that from one new moon to another, and from one Sabbath to another, shall all flesh come to worship before me, saith the LORD" (Isaiah 66:8, 9, 18-20, 23).

"10 Sing and rejoice, O daughter of Zion: for, lo, I come, and I will dwell in the midst of thee, saith the LORD. And many nations shall be joined to the LORD in that day, and shall be my people: and I will dwell in the midst of thee, and thou shalt know that the LORD of hosts hath sent me unto thee" (Zechariah 2:10, 11).

"And in the days of these kings shall the God of heaven set up a kingdom, which shall never be destroyed: and the kingdom shall not be left to other people, but it shall break in pieces and consume all these kingdoms, and it shall stand for ever" (Daniel 2:44).

"I saw in the night visions, and, behold, one like the Son of man came with the clouds of heaven, and came to the Ancient of days, and they brought him near before him. And there was given him dominion, and glory, and a kingdom, that all people, nations, and languages, should serve him: his dominion is an everlasting dominion, which shall not pass away, and his kingdom that which shall not be destroyed. And the kingdom and dominion, and the greatness of the kingdom under the whole heaven, shall be given to the people of the saints of the most High, whose kingdom is an everlasting kingdom, and all dominions shall serve and obey him" (Daniel 7:13, 14, 27).

"And the LORD shall be king over all the earth: in that day shall there be one LORD, and his name one" (Zechariah 14:9).

"I say unto you, That many shall come from the east and west, and shall sit down with Abraham, and Isaac, and Jacob, in the kingdom of heaven" (Matthew 8:11).

"In that day will I raise up the tabernacle of David that is fallen, and close up the breaches thereof; and I will raise up his ruins, and I will build it as in the days of old: that they may possess the remnant of Edom [or, that the residue of men might seek after the Lord, Acts 15:17], and of all the heathen, which are called by my name, saith the LORD that doeth this" (Amos 9:11, 12).

"When thou shalt make his soul an offering for sin, he shall see his seed, he shall prolong his days, and the pleasure of the LORD shall prosper in his hand. He shall see of the travail of his soul, and shall be satisfied: by his knowledge shall my righteous servant justify many; for he shall bear their iniquities. Therefore will I divide him a portion with the great, and he shall divide the spoil with the strong" (Isaiah 53:10-12).

"And I, if I be lifted up from the earth, will draw all men unto me" (John 12:32).

"And they that are far off shall come and build in the temple of the LORD" (Zechariah 6:15).

"Behold, I create new heavens and a new earth: and the former shall not be remembered, nor come into mind" (Isaiah 65:17).

"From the rising of the sun even unto the going down of the same my name shall be great among the Gentiles; and in every place incense shall be offered unto my name, and a pure offering: for my name shall be great among the heathen, saith the LORD of hosts" (Malachi 1:11).

"And the inhabitants of one city shall go to another, saying, Let us go speedily to pray before the LORD, and to seek the LORD of hosts: I will go also. Yea, many people and strong nations shall come to seek the LORD of hosts in Jerusalem, and to pray before the LORD. Thus saith the LORD of hosts; In those days it shall come to pass, that ten men shall take hold out of all languages of the nations, even shall take hold of the skirt of him that is a Jew, saying, We will go with you: for we have heard that God is with you" (Zechariah 8:21-23).

"And the seventh angel sounded; and there were great voices in heaven, saying, The kingdoms of this world are become the kingdoms of our Lord, and of his Christ; and he shall reign for ever and ever" (Revelation 11:15). See Rev. 7:9, 10; 12:10.

2. Glory Of The Church

"And he carried me away in the spirit to a great and high mountain, and shewed me that great city, the holy Jerusalem, descending out of heaven from God, having the glory of God: and her light was like unto a stone most precious, even like a jasper stone, clear as crystal. [See verses 18, 21.] And I saw no temple therein: for the Lord God Almighty and the Lamb are the temple of it. And the city had no need of the sun, neither of the moon, to shine in it: for the glory of God did lighten it, and the Lamb is the light thereof. And the nations of them which are saved shall walk in the light of it: and the kings of the earth do bring their glory and honour into it. And the gates of it shall not be shut at all by day: for there shall be no night there. And they shall bring the glory and honour of the nations into it" (Revelation 21:10, 11, 22-26).

"The king's daughter is all glorious within: her clothing is of wrought gold" (Psalm 45:13).

"O thou afflicted, tossed with tempest, and not comforted, behold, I will lay thy stones with fair colours, and lay thy foundations with sapphires. And I will make thy windows of agates, and thy gates of carbuncles, and all thy borders of pleasant stones" (Isaiah 54:11, 12).

"Arise, shine; for thy light is come, and the glory of the LORD is risen upon thee. For, behold, the darkness shall cover the earth, and gross darkness the people: but the LORD shall arise upon thee, and his glory shall be seen upon thee. The glory of Lebanon shall come unto thee, the fir tree, the pine tree, and the box together, to beautify the place of my sanctuary; and I will make the place of my feet glorious. Whereas thou hast been forsaken and hated, so that no man went through thee, I will make thee an eternal excellency, a joy of many generations. The sun shall be no more thy light by day; neither for brightness shall the moon give light unto thee: but the LORD shall be unto thee an everlasting light, and thy God thy glory" (Isaiah 60:1, 2, 13, 15, 19).

"Glorious things are spoken of thee, O city of God" (Psalm 87:3).

"I bring near my righteousness; it shall not be far off, and my salvation shall not tarry: and I will place salvation in Zion for Israel my glory" (Isaiah 46:13).

"The Gentiles shall see thy righteousness, and all kings thy glory: and thou shalt be called by a new name, which the mouth of the LORD shall name. Thou shalt also be a crown of glory in the hand of the LORD, and a royal diadem in the hand of thy God" (Isaiah 62:2, 3).

"Beautiful for situation, the joy of the whole earth, is mount Zion, on the sides of the north, the city of the great King. Walk about Zion, and go round about her: tell the towers thereof. Mark ye well her bulwarks, consider her palaces; that ye may tell it to the generation following" (Psalm 48:2, 12, 13).

3. Increase Of Light And Knowledge, And Of The Means Of Grace

"And all thy children shall be taught of the LORD" (Isaiah 54:13).

"Many shall run to and fro, and knowledge shall be increased" (Daniel 12:4).

"The earth shall be full of the knowledge of the LORD, as the waters cover the sea" (Isaiah 11:9).

"And in this mountain shall the LORD of hosts make unto all people a feast of fat things, a feast of wines on the lees, of fat things full of marrow, of wines on the lees well refined. And he will destroy in this mountain the face of the covering cast over all people, and the vail that is spread over all nations" (Isaiah 25:6, 7).

"I will open rivers in high places, and fountains in the midst of the valleys: I will make the wilderness a pool of water, and the dry land springs of water. I will plant in the wilderness the cedar, the shittah tree, and the myrtle, and the oil tree; I will set in the desert the fir tree, and the pine, and the box tree together" (Isaiah 41:18, 19). See Isa. 35:6-8.

"How beautiful upon the mountains are the feet of him that bringeth good tidings, that publisheth peace; that bringeth good tidings of good, that publisheth salvation; that saith unto Zion, Thy God reigneth! Thy watchmen shall lift up the voice; with the voice together shall they sing: for they shall see eye to eye, when the LORD shall bring again Zion" (Isaiah 52:7, 8).

"In that day shall the deaf hear the words of the book, and the eyes of the blind shall see out of obscurity, and out of darkness. They also that erred in spirit shall come to understanding, and they that murmured shall learn doctrine" (Isaiah 29:18, 24).

4. Increase Of Purity, Holiness, And Righteousness

"The LORD is exalted; for he dwelleth on high: he hath filled Zion with judgment and righteousness. And wisdom and knowledge shall be the stability of thy times, and strength of salvation: the fear of the LORD is his treasure" (Isaiah 33:5, 6).

"Thy people also shall be all righteous: they shall inherit the land for ever, the branch of my planting, the work of my hands, that I may be glorified" (Isaiah 60:21).

"And it shall come to pass, that he that is left in Zion, and he that remaineth in Jerusalem, shall be called holy, even every one that is written among the living in Jerusalem: when the Lord shall have washed away the filth of the daughters of Zion, and shall have purged the blood of Jerusalem from the midst thereof by the spirit of judgment, and by the spirit of burning" (Isaiah 4:3, 4).

"And to her [the Lamb's wife] was granted that she should be arrayed in fine linen, clean and white: for the fine linen is the righteousness of saints" (Revelation 19:8).

"Until the spirit be poured upon us from on high, and the wilderness be a fruitful field, and the fruitful field be counted for a forest. Then judgment shall dwell in the wilderness, and righteousness remain in the fruitful field" (Isaiah 32:15, 16).

"He shall sit as a refiner and purifier of silver: and he shall purify the sons of Levi, and purge them as gold and silver, that they may offer unto the LORD an offering in righteousness. Then shall the offering of Judah and Jerusalem be pleasant unto the LORD, as in the days of old, and as in former years" (Malachi 3:3, 4).

"In that day shall there be upon the bells of the horses, HOLINESS UNTO THE LORD; and the pots in the LORD'S house shall be like the bowls before the altar. Yea, every pot in Jerusalem and in Judah shall be holiness unto the LORD of hosts: and all they that sacrifice shall come and take of them, and seethe therein: and in that day there shall be no more the Canaanite in the house of the LORD of hosts" (Zechariah 14:20, 21).

"They shall fear thee as long as the sun and moon endure, throughout all generations" (Psalm 72:5).

"Drop down, ye heavens, from above, and let the skies pour down righteousness: let the earth open, and let them bring forth salvation, and let righteousness spring up together; I the LORD have created it" (Isaiah 45:8).

"As the earth bringeth forth her bud, and as the garden causeth the things that are sown in it to spring forth; so the Lord GOD will cause righteousness and praise to spring forth before all the nations" (Isaiah 61:11).

"Mercy and truth are met together; righteousness and peace have kissed each other. Truth shall spring out of the earth; and righteousness shall look down from heaven. Righteousness shall go before him; and shall set us in the way of his steps" (Psalm 85:10, 11, 13).

5. Peace, Love And Unity

"And they shall beat their swords into plowshares, and their spears into pruninghooks: nation shall not lift up sword against nation, neither shall they learn war any more" (Isaiah 2:4).

"Neither pray I for these alone, but for them also which shall believe on me through their word; that they all may be one; as thou, Father, art in me, and I in thee, that they also may be one in us: that the world may believe that thou hast sent me. And the glory which thou gavest me I have given them; that they may be one, even as we are one: I in them, and thou in me, that they may be made perfect in one; and that the world may know that thou hast sent me, and hast loved them, as thou hast loved me" (John 17:20-23).

"The wolf also shall dwell with the lamb, and the leopard shall lie down with the kid; and the calf and the young lion and the fatling together; and a little child shall lead them. And the cow and the bear shall feed; their young ones shall lie down together: and the lion shall eat straw like the ox. And the sucking child shall play on the hole of the asp, and the weaned child shall put his hand on the cockatrice' den. They shall not hurt nor destroy in all my holy mountain. The envy also of Ephraim shall depart, and the adversaries of Judah shall be cut off: Ephraim shall not envy Judah, and Judah shall not vex Ephraim" (Isaiah 11:6-9, 13).

"The mountains shall bring peace to the people, and the little hills, by righteousness. In his days shall the righteous flourish; and abundance of peace so long as the moon endureth" (Psalm 72:3, 7).

"From whom [Christ] the whole body fitly joined together and compacted by that which every joint supplieth, according to the effectual working in the measure of every part, maketh increase of the body unto the edifying of itself in love" (Ephesians 4:16).

6. Submission And Destruction Of The Enemies Of The Church

"In that day the LORD with his sore and great and strong sword shall punish leviathan the piercing serpent, even leviathan that crooked serpent; and he shall slay the dragon that is in the sea" (Isaiah 27:1).

"The LORD shall send the rod of thy strength out of Zion: rule thou in the midst of thine enemies. The Lord at thy right hand shall strike through kings in the day of his wrath. He shall judge among the heathen, he shall fill the places with the dead bodies; he shall wound the heads over many countries" (Psalm 110:2, 5, 6).

"When the enemy shall come in like a flood, the Spirit of the LORD shall lift up a standard against him" (Isaiah 59:19).

"He shall smite the earth with the rod of his mouth, and with the breath of his lips shall he slay the wicked" (Isaiah 11:4).

"Behold, all they that were incensed against thee shall be ashamed and confounded: they shall be as nothing; and they that strive with thee shall perish. Thou shalt seek them, and shalt not find them, even them that contended with thee: they that war against thee shall be as nothing, and as a thing of nought" (Isaiah 41:11, 12). See verses 15, 16.

"Shall the prey be taken from the mighty, or the lawful captive delivered? But thus saith the LORD, Even the captives of the mighty shall be taken away, and the prey of the terrible shall be delivered: for I will contend with him that contendeth with thee, and I will save thy children. And I will feed them that oppress thee with their own flesh; and they shall be drunken with their own blood, as with sweet wine: and all flesh shall know that I the LORD am thy Saviour and thy Redeemer, the mighty One of Jacob" (Isaiah 49:24-26).

"The sons also of them that afflicted thee shall come bending unto thee; and all they that despised thee shall bow themselves down at the soles of thy feet; and they shall call thee, The city of the LORD, The Zion of the Holy One of Israel" (Isaiah 60:14).

The destruction of antichrist, babylon, etc.

"Then shall that Wicked be revealed, whom the Lord shall consume with the spirit of his mouth, and shall destroy with the brightness of his coming" (2Thessalonians 2:8). See Dan. 7:24-26.

"If any man worship the beast and his image, and receive his mark in his forehead, or in his hand, the same shall drink of the wine of the wrath of God, which is poured out without mixture into the cup of his indignation" (Revelation 14:9, 10).

"For thus saith the Lord GOD; When I shall make thee a desolate city, like the cities that are not inhabited; when I shall bring up the deep upon thee, and great waters shall cover thee; I will make thee a terror, and thou shalt be no more: though thou be sought for, yet shalt thou never be found again, saith the Lord GOD" (Ezekiel 26:19, 21).

"Babylon the great is fallen, is fallen, and is become the habitation of devils, and the hold of every foul spirit, and a cage of every unclean and hateful bird" (Revelation 18:2). See to the end of the chapter.

"And I saw the beast, and the kings of the earth, and their armies, gathered together to make war against Him that sat on the horse, and against his army. 20 And the beast was taken, and with him the false prophet that wrought miracles before him, with which he deceived them that had received the mark of the beast, and them that worshipped his image. These both were cast alive into a lake of fire burning with brimstone" (Revelation 19:19, 20).

"And when the thousand years are expired, Satan shall be loosed out of his prison, and shall go out to deceive the nations which are in the four quarters of the earth, Gog and Magog, to gather them together to battle: the number of whom is as the sand of the sea. And they went up on the breadth of the earth, and compassed the camp of the saints about, and the beloved city: and fire came down from God out of heaven, and devoured them" (Revelation 20:7-9). See Ezek. 38, 39.

7. Favor And Submission Of Kings To The Kingdom Of Christ

"So shall he sprinkle many nations; the kings shall shut their mouths at him: for that which had not been told them shall they see; and that which they had not heard shall they consider" (Isaiah 52:15).

"Thus saith the LORD, the Redeemer of Israel, and his Holy One, to him whom man despiseth, to him whom the nation abhorreth, to a servant of rulers, Kings shall see and arise, princes also shall worship, because of the LORD that is faithful, and the Holy One of Israel, and he shall choose thee. And kings shall be thy nursing fathers, and their queens thy nursing mothers: they shall bow down to thee with their face toward the earth, and lick up the dust of thy feet; and thou shalt know that I am the LORD: for they shall not be ashamed that wait for me" (Isaiah 49:7, 23).

"And the Gentiles shall come to thy light, and kings to the brightness of thy rising. And the sons of strangers shall build up thy walls, and their kings shall minister unto thee: for in my wrath I smote thee, but in my favour have I had mercy on thee. Therefore thy gates shall be open continually; they shall not be shut day nor night; that men may bring unto thee the forces of the Gentiles, and that their kings may be brought. Thou shalt also suck the milk of the Gentiles, and shalt suck the breast of kings: and thou shalt know that I the LORD am thy Saviour and thy Redeemer, the mighty One of Jacob" (Isaiah 60:3, 10, 11, 16).

8. The Security, Tranquility, And Prosperity Of The Church

"The LORD shall comfort Zion: he will comfort all her waste places; and he will make her wilderness like Eden, and her desert like the garden of the LORD; joy and gladness shall be found therein, thanksgiving, and the voice of melody" (Isaiah 51:3).

"Look upon Zion, the city of our solemnities: thine eyes shall see Jerusalem a quiet habitation, a tabernacle that shall not be taken down; not one of the stakes thereof shall ever be removed, neither shall any of the cords thereof be broken. But there the glorious LORD will be unto us a place of broad rivers and streams;

wherein shall go no galley with oars, neither shall gallant ship pass thereby. For the LORD is our judge, the LORD is our lawgiver, the LORD is our king; he will save us" (Isaiah 33:20-22).

"Upon this rock I will build my church; and the gates of hell shall not prevail against it" (Matthew 16:18).

"In righteousness shalt thou be established: thou shalt be far from oppression; for thou shalt not fear: and from terror; for it shall not come near thee. Behold, they shall surely gather together, but not by me: whosoever shall gather together against thee shall fall for thy sake. No weapon that is formed against thee shall prosper; and every tongue that shall rise against thee in judgment thou shalt condemn. This is the heritage of the servants of the LORD, and their righteousness is of me, saith the LORD" (Isaiah 54:14, 15, 17).

"Rejoice ye with Jerusalem, and be glad with her, all ye that love her: rejoice for joy with her, all ye that mourn for her: that ye may suck, and be satisfied with the breasts of her consolations; that ye may milk out, and be delighted with the abundance of her glory. For thus saith the LORD, Behold, I will extend peace to her like a river, and the glory of the Gentiles like a flowing stream: then shall ye suck, ye shall be borne upon her sides, and be dandled upon her knees" (Isaiah 66:10-12). See verses 13, 14.

"In those days shall Judah be saved, and Jerusalem shall dwell safely" (Jeremiah 33:16).

"In that day sing ye unto her, A vineyard of red wine. I the LORD do keep it; I will water it every moment: lest any hurt it, I will keep it night and day" (Isaiah 27:2, 3).

"And the kingdom and dominion, and the greatness of the kingdom under the whole heaven, shall be given to the people of the saints of the Most High, whose kingdom is an everlasting kingdom, and all dominions shall serve and obey him" (Daniel 7:27).

"Thou shalt arise, and have mercy upon Zion: for the time to favour her, yea, the set time, is come. For thy servants take pleasure in her stones, and favour the dust thereof. When the LORD shall build up Zion, he shall appear in his glory" (Psalm 102:13, 14, 16).

"And the LORD will create upon every dwelling place of mount Zion, and upon her assemblies, a cloud and smoke by day, and the shining of a flaming fire by night: for upon all the glory shall be a defence. And there shall be a tabernacle for a shadow in the daytime from the heat, and for a place of refuge, and for a covert from storm and from rain" (Isaiah 4:5, 6).

"Be ye glad and rejoice for ever in that which I create: for, behold, I create Jerusalem a rejoicing, and her people a joy. And I will rejoice in Jerusalem, and joy in my people: and the voice of weeping shall be no more heard in her, nor the voice of crying" (Isaiah 65:18, 19).

9. The Perpetual Continuance Of The Church

"For as the new heavens and the new earth, which I will make, shall remain before me, saith the LORD, so shall your seed and your name remain" (Isaiah 66:22).

"Thus saith the LORD, which giveth the sun for a light by day, and the ordinances of the moon and of the stars for a light by night, which divideth the sea when the waves thereof roar; The LORD of hosts is his name: If those ordinances depart from before me, saith the LORD, then the seed of Israel also shall cease from being a nation before me for ever. Thus saith the LORD; If heaven above can be measured, and the foundations of the earth searched out beneath, I will also cast off all the seed of Israel for all that they have done, saith the LORD" (Jeremiah 31:35-37). See Jer. 33:20-22, 25, 26.

"Lo, I am with you alway, even unto the end of the world" (Matthew 28:20).

"He shall reign over the house of Jacob for ever; and of his kingdom there shall be no end" (Luke 1:33).

"His dominion is an everlasting dominion, which shall not pass away, and his kingdom that which shall not be destroyed" (Daniel 7:14).

"The kingdoms of this world are become the kingdoms of our Lord, and of his Christ; and he shall reign for ever and ever" (Revelation 11:15).

"In the days of these kings shall the God of heaven set up a kingdom, which shall never be destroyed: and the kingdom shall not be left to other people, but it shall break in pieces and consume all these kingdoms, and it shall stand for ever" (Daniel 2:44).

"As for me, this is my covenant with them, saith the LORD; My spirit that is upon thee, and my words which I have put in thy mouth, shall not depart out of thy mouth, nor out of the mouth of thy seed, nor out of the mouth of thy seed's seed, saith the LORD, from henceforth and for ever" (Isaiah 59:21).

10. The Conversion And Restoration Of The Jews

"And men shall dwell in it [that is, all the land], and there shall be no more utter destruction; but Jerusalem shall be safely inhabited" (Zechariah 14:11). See the whole chapter.

"Nevertheless I will remember my covenant with thee in the days of thy youth, and I will establish unto thee an everlasting covenant. Then thou shalt remember thy ways, and be ashamed, when thou shalt receive thy sisters, thine elder and thy younger [Sodom and Samaria, verse 55]: and I will give them unto thee for daughters, but not by thy covenant" (Ezekiel 16:60, 61). See also verses 62, 63.

"Yet the number of the children of Israel shall be as the sand of the sea, which cannot be measured nor numbered; and it shall come to pass, that in the place where it was said unto them, Ye are not my people, there it shall be said unto them, Ye are the sons of the living God. Then shall the children of Judah and the children of Israel be gathered together, and appoint themselves one head, and they shall come up out of the land: for great shall be the day of Jezreel" (Hosea 1:10, 11).

"And I will cause the captivity of Judah and the captivity of Israel to return, and will build them, as at the first. And I will cleanse them from all their iniquity, whereby they have sinned against me; and I will pardon all their iniquities, whereby they have sinned, and whereby they have transgressed against me. And it shall be to me a name of joy, a praise and an honour before all the nations of the earth, which shall hear all the good that I do unto them: and they shall fear and tremble for all the goodness and for all the prosperity that I procure unto it. In those days, and at that time, will I cause the Branch of righteousness to grow up unto David; and he shall execute judgment and righteousness in the land. In those days shall Judah be saved, and Jerusalem shall dwell safely: and this is the name wherewith she shall be called, The LORD our righteousness. Considerest thou not what this people have spoken, saying, The two families which the LORD hath chosen, he hath even cast them off? thus they have despised my people, that they should be no more a nation before them. Thus saith the LORD; If my covenant be not with day and night, and if I have not appointed the ordinances of heaven and earth; then will I cast away the seed of Jacob, and David my servant, so that I will not take any of his seed to be rulers over the seed of Abraham, Isaac, and Jacob: for I will cause their captivity to return, and have mercy on them" (Jeremiah 33:7-9, 15, 16, 24-26). To the same purpose see the whole chapter. See also Chapter 50:4, 5, 19, 20.

"I will surely assemble, O Jacob, all of thee; I will surely gather the remnant of Israel; I will put them together as the sheep of Bozrah, as the flock in the midst of their fold: they shall make great noise by reason of the multitude of men. The breaker is come up before them: they have broken up, and have passed through the gate, and are gone out by it: and their king shall pass before them, and the LORD on the head of them" (Micah 2:12, 13).

"I will multiply upon you [the mountains of Israel] man and beast; and they shall increase and bring fruit: and I will settle you after your old estates, and will do better unto you than at your beginnings: and ye shall know that I am the LORD. I will take you from among the heathen, and gather you out of all countries, and will bring you into your own land. Then will I sprinkle clean water upon you, and ye shall be clean: from all your filthiness, and from all your idols, will I cleanse you. A new heart also will I give you, and a new spirit will I put within you: and I will take away the stony heart out of your flesh, and I will give you an heart of flesh. In the day that I shall have cleansed you from all your iniquities I will also cause you to dwell in the cities, and the wastes shall be builded" (Ezekiel 36:11, 24-26, 33). See the whole chapter; also Chapter 37.

"Jerusalem shall be trodden down of the Gentiles, until the times of the Gentiles be fulfilled" (Luke 21:24).

"And they shall dwell in the land that I have given unto Jacob my servant, wherein your fathers have dwelt; and they shall dwell therein, even they, and their children, and their children's children for ever: and my servant David shall be their prince for ever" (Ezekiel 37:25).

"I will bring you out from the people, and will gather you out of the countries wherein ye are scattered, with a mighty hand, and with a stretched out arm, and with fury poured out. And I will bring you into the wilderness of the people, and there will I plead with you face to face. And I will cause you to pass under the rod, and I will bring you into the bond of the covenant: And I will purge out from among you the rebels, and them that transgress against me: In mine holy mountain, in the mountain of the height of Israel, saith the Lord GOD, there shall all the house of Israel, all of them in the land, serve me: there will I accept them, and there will I require your offerings, and the firstfruits of your oblations, with all your holy things" (Ezekiel 20:34, 35, 37, 38,

40). See also verses 41, 44.

"Yea, I will rejoice over them to do them good, and I will plant them in this land assuredly with my whole heart and with my whole soul" (Jeremiah 32:41). See from verse 37 to the end.

"And I will set up one shepherd over them, and he shall feed them, even my servant David; he shall feed them, and he shall be their shepherd. And I the LORD will be their God, and my servant David a prince among them; I the LORD have spoken it. And they shall no more be a prey to the heathen, neither shall the beast of the land devour them; but they shall dwell safely, and none shall make them afraid. And I will raise up for them a plant of renown" (Ezekiel 34:23, 24, 28, 29). See also verses 11, 16, and from verse 22 to the end of the chapter.

"Behold, I will allure her, and bring her into the wilderness, and speak comfortably unto her. And I will give her her vineyards from thence, and the valley of Achor for a door of hope: and she shall sing there, as in the days of her youth, and as in the day when she came up out of the land of Egypt. And I will betroth thee unto me for ever; yea, I will betroth thee unto me in righteousness, and in judgment, and in lovingkindness, and in mercies" (Hosea 2:14, 15, 19). See from verse 16 to the end.

"Even unto this day, when Moses is read, the vail is upon their heart. Nevertheless when it shall turn to the Lord, the vail shall be taken away" (2Corinthians 3:15, 16).

"Sing and rejoice, O daughter of Zion: for, lo, I come, and I will dwell in the midst of thee, saith the LORD. And the LORD shall inherit Judah his portion in the holy land, and shall choose Jerusalem again" (Zechariah 2:10, 12).

"Therefore will he give them up, until the time that she which travaileth hath brought forth: then the remnant of his brethren shall return unto the children of Israel. And he shall stand and feed in the strength of the LORD, in the majesty of the name of the LORD his God; and they shall abide: for now shall he be great unto the ends of the earth. And the remnant of Jacob shall be in the midst of many people as a dew from the LORD, as the showers upon the grass, that tarrieth not for man, nor waiteth for the sons of men. Thy graven images also will I cut off, and thy standing images out of the midst of thee; and thou shalt no more worship the work of thine hands" (Micah 5:3, 4, 7, 13). See the whole chapter, Chapter 4, and Chapter 7:14, 17. See also Zeph. 3:9, to the end.

"Upon mount Zion shall be deliverance, and there shall be holiness; and the house of Jacob shall possess their possessions. And saviours shall come up on mount Zion to judge the mount of Esau; and the kingdom shall be the LORD'S" (Obadiah 1:17, 21).

"The children of Israel shall abide many days without a king, and without a prince, and without a sacrifice, and without an image, and without an ephod, and without teraphim: Afterward shall the children of Israel return, and seek the LORD their God, and David their king; and shall fear the LORD and his goodness in the latter days" (Hosea 3:4, 5).

"Behold, in those days, and in that time, when I shall bring again the captivity of Judah and Jerusalem, I will also gather all nations, and will bring them down into the valley of Jehoshaphat, and will plead with them there for my people and for my heritage Israel, whom they have scattered among the nations, and parted my land. So shall ye know that I am the LORD your God dwelling in Zion, my holy mountain: then shall Jerusalem be holy, and there shall no strangers pass through her any more. Judah shall dwell for ever, and Jerusalem from generation to generation" (Joel 3:1, 2, 17, 20). See also verses 7, 14, 16, 18, 21.

"And I will strengthen the house of Judah, and I will save the house of Joseph, and I will bring them again to place them; for I have mercy upon them: and they shall be as though I had not cast them off: for I am the LORD their God, and will hear them. I will hiss for them, and gather them; for I have redeemed them: and they shall increase as they have increased. And I will sow them among the people: and they shall remember me in far countries; and they shall live with their children, and turn again" (Zechariah 10:6, 8, 9). See the whole chapter.

"God hath not cast away his people which he foreknew. If the fall of them be the riches of the world, and the diminishing of them the riches of the Gentiles; how much more their fulness? For if the casting away of them be the reconciling of the world, what shall the receiving of them be, but life from the dead? And they also, if they abide not still in unbelief, shall be graffed in: for God is able to graff them in again. How much more shall these, which be the natural branches, be graffed into their own olive tree? For I would not, brethren, that ye should be ignorant of this mystery, lest ye should be wise in your own conceits; that blindness in part is happened to Israel, until the fulness of the Gentiles be come in. And so all Israel shall be saved: as it is written, There shall come out of Sion the Deliverer, and shall turn away ungodliness from Jacob: for this is my covenant unto them, when I shall take away their sins. As concerning the gospel, they are enemies for your sakes: but as touching the election, they are beloved for the Father's sakes. For the gifts and calling of God are without repentance. [See also verses 30-31.] God hath concluded them all in unbelief, that he might have mercy upon all. O the depth of the riches both of the wisdom and knowledge of God! how unsearchable are his judgments, and his ways past finding out!" (Romans 11:2, 12, 15, 23, 24, 25-29, 32-33).

"At the same time, saith the LORD, will I be the God of all the families of Israel, and they shall be my people. Again I will build thee, and thou shalt be built, O virgin of Israel: thou shalt again be adorned with thy tabrets, and shalt go forth in the dances of them that make merry. Hear the word of the LORD, O ye nations, and declare it in the isles afar off, and say, He that scattered Israel will gather him, and keep him, as a shepherd doth his flock. There is hope in thine end, saith the LORD, that thy children shall come again to their own border. Behold, the days come, saith the LORD, that I will make a new covenant with the house of Israel, and with the house of Judah: not according to the covenant that I made with their fathers in the day that I took them by the hand to bring them out of the land of Egypt; which my covenant they brake, although I was an husband unto them, saith the LORD: But this shall be the covenant that I will make with the house of Israel; After those days, saith the LORD, I will put my law in their inward parts, and write it in their hearts; and will be their God, and they shall be my people. Behold, the days come, saith the LORD, that the city shall be built to the LORD from the tower of Hananeel unto the gate of the corner" (Jeremiah 31:1, 4, 10, 17, 31-33, 38). See the whole chapter.

"In that day will I make the governors of Judah like an hearth of fire among the wood, and like a torch of fire in a sheaf; and they shall devour all the people round about, on the right hand and on the left: and Jerusalem shall be inhabited again in her own place, even in Jerusalem. And I will pour upon the house of David, and upon the inhabitants of Jerusalem, the spirit of grace and of supplications: and they shall look upon me whom they have pierced, and they shall mourn for him, as one mourneth for his only son, and shall be in bitterness for him, as one that is in bitterness for his firstborn" (Zechariah 12:6, 10). See the whole chapter.

"And I will bring again the captivity of my people of Israel, and they shall build the waste cities, and inhabit them. And I will plant them upon their land, and they shall no more be pulled up out of their land which I have given them, saith the LORD thy God" (Amos 9:14, 15).

"They shall serve the LORD their God, and David their king, whom I will raise up unto them. Therefore fear thou not, O my servant Jacob, saith the LORD; neither be dismayed, O Israel: for, lo, I will save thee from afar, and thy seed from the land of their captivity; and Jacob shall return, and shall be in rest, and be quiet, and none shall make him afraid" (Jeremiah 30:9, 10). See to the end of the chapter.

PART FOUR

Promises Of Christ's Second Coming -- That Christ Will Come Again

"Judge nothing before the time, until the Lord come, who both will bring to light the hidden things of darkness, and will make manifest the counsels of the hearts" (1Corinthians 4:5).

"Henceforth there is laid up for me a crown of righteousness, which the Lord, the righteous Judge, shall give me at that day: and not to me only, but unto all them also that love his appearing" (2Timothy 4:8).

"The Lord himself shall descend from heaven with a shout, with the voice of the archangel, and with the trump of God: and the dead in Christ shall rise first: then we which are alive and remain shall be caught up together with them in the clouds, to meet the Lord in the air: and so shall we ever be with the Lord" (1Thessalonians 4:16, 17).

"Watch therefore: for ye know not what hour your Lord doth come" (Matthew 24:42).

"Ye have heard how I said unto you, I go away, and come again unto you" (John 14:28).

"To wait for his Son from heaven, whom he raised from the dead, even Jesus, which delivered us from the wrath to come" (1Thessalonians 1:10).

"They shall look upon me whom they have pierced, and they shall mourn for him" (Zechariah 12:10).

"When Christ, who is our life, shall appear, then shall ye also appear with him in glory" (Colossians 3:4).

"I know that my Redeemer liveth, and that he shall stand at the latter day upon the earth" (Job 19:25).

"And his feet shall stand in that day upon the mount of Olives, which is before Jerusalem" (Zechariah 14:4).

"As often as ye eat this bread, and drink this cup, ye do shew the Lord's death till he come" (1Corinthians 11:26).

"The Lord direct your hearts into the love of God, and into the patient waiting for Christ" (2Thessalonians 3:5).

"They shall see the Son of man coming in the clouds of heaven with power and great glory" (Matthew 24:30).

"We know that, when he shall appear, we shall be like him; for we shall see him as he is" (1John 3:2).

"When the Chief Shepherd shall appear, ye shall receive a crown of glory that fadeth not away" (1Peter 5:4).

"Behold, he cometh with clouds; and every eye shall see him, and they also which pierced him" (Revelation 1:7).

"Ye shall see the Son of man sitting on the right hand of power, and coming in the clouds of heaven" (Mark 14:62).

"To you who are troubled rest with us, when the Lord Jesus shall be revealed from heaven with his mighty angels" (2Thessalonians 1:7).

"If I go and prepare a place for you, I will come again, and receive you unto myself; that where I am, there ye may be also" (John 14:3).

"As the lightning cometh out of the east, and shineth even unto the west; so shall also the coming of the Son of man be" (Matthew 24:27).

"Looking for that blessed hope, and the glorious appearing of the great God and our Saviour Jesus Christ" (Titus 2:13).

"This same Jesus, which is taken up from you into heaven, shall so come in like manner as ye have seen him go into heaven" (Acts 1:11).

"The Son of man shall come in the glory of his Father with his angels; and then he shall reward every man according to his works" (Matthew 16:27).

"When the Son of man shall come in his glory, and all the holy angels with him, then shall he sit upon the throne of his glory" (Matthew 25:31).

"He shall send Jesus Christ, which before was preached unto you: whom the heaven must receive until the times of restitution of all things" (Acts 3:20, 21).

"So Christ was once offered to bear the sins of many; and unto them that look for him shall he appear the second time without sin unto salvation" (Hebrews 9:28).

"Behold, I come quickly; and my reward is with me, to give every man according as his work shall be... Amen. Even so, come, Lord Jesus" (Revelation 22:12, 20).

"To the end he may stablish your hearts unblameable in holiness before God, even our Father, at the coming of our Lord Jesus Christ with all his saints" (1Thessalonians 3:13).

"Waiting for the coming of our Lord Jesus Christ: who shall also confirm you unto the end, that ye may be blameless in the day of our Lord" (1Corinthians 1:7, 8).

"I saw in the night visions, and, behold, one like the Son of man came with the clouds of heaven... and there was given him dominion, and glory, and a kingdom... which shall not be destroyed" (Daniel 7:13, 14).

"Our conversation is in heaven; from whence also we look for the Saviour, the Lord Jesus Christ: who shall change our vile body... according to the working whereby he is able even to subdue all things unto himself" (Philippians 3:20, 21).

"There shall come in the last days scoffers, walking after their own lusts, and saying, Where is the promise of his coming? for since the fathers fell asleep, all things continue as they were from the beginning of the creation... But the day of the Lord will come as a thief in the night" (2Peter 3:3, 4, 10).

CONCLUSION

That God Will Perform All His Promises

"Know therefore that the LORD thy God, he is God, the faithful God, which keepeth covenant and mercy with them that love him and keep his commandments to a thousand generations" (Deuteronomy 7:9).

"For ever, O LORD, thy word is settled in heaven. Thy faithfulness is unto all generations. Thy word is true from the beginning" (Psalm 119:89, 90, 160).

"God is not a man, that he should lie; neither the son of man, that he should repent: hath he said, and shall he not do it? or hath he spoken, and shall he not make it good?" (Numbers 23:19).

"That by two immutable things, in which it was impossible for God to lie, we might have a strong consolation, who have fled for refuge to lay hold upon the hope set before us" (Hebrews 6:18).

"The word of the LORD is tried" (Psalm 18:30).

"He is faithful that promised" (Hebrews 10:23).

"Thy counsels of old are faithfulness and truth" (Isaiah 25:1).

"My covenant will I not break, nor alter the thing that is gone out of my lips" (Psalm 89:34).

"I have spoken it, I will also bring it to pass; I have purposed it, I will also do it" (Isaiah 46:11).

"He hath remembered his covenant for ever, the word which he commanded to a thousand generations" (Psalm 105:8).

"Ye know in all your hearts and in all your souls, that not one thing hath failed of all the good things which the LORD your God spake concerning you; all are come to pass unto you, and not one thing hath failed thereof" (Joshua 23:14). See also 1Kings 8:56.

"The mountains shall depart, and the hills be removed; but my kindness shall not depart from thee, neither shall the covenant of my peace be removed, saith the LORD that hath mercy on thee" (Isaiah 54:10).

"If we believe not, yet he abideth faithful: he cannot deny himself" (2Timothy 2:13).

"The Lord is not slack concerning his promise, as some men count slackness" (2Peter 3:9).

"Being fully persuaded that, what he had promised, he was able also to perform" (Romans 4:21).

"All the promises of God in him are yea, and in him Amen, unto the glory of God" (2Corinthians 1:20).

"In hope of eternal life, which God, that cannot lie, promised before the world began" (Titus 1:2).

"The Strength of Israel will not lie nor repent: for he is not a man, that he should repent" (1Samuel 15:29).

"He will not forsake thee... nor forget the covenant of thy fathers which he sware unto them" (Deuteronomy 4:31).

"They that know thy name will put their trust in thee: for thou, LORD, hast not forsaken them that seek thee" (Psalm 9:10).

"Whereby are given unto us exceeding great and precious promises" (2Peter 1:4).

Made in the USA
San Bernardino, CA
28 December 2018